T0098016

RECIPES FROM MY
DUTCH KITCHEN

RECIPES FROM MY
DUTCH KITCHEN

Explore the unique and delicious cuisine of the Netherlands in over 80 classic dishes

JANNY DE MOOR

with photographs by Debi Treloar

aquamarine

Front cover *High Moorland Leg of Lamb (see pages 102–3);* **page 1** *Herring Salad (see pages 28–9);* **page 2** *Groningen Prawn Soup (see pages 48–9);* **page 3** *Meat Croquettes (see pages 38–9);* **this page** *Stone Pudding (see pages 32–3);* **opposite left** *Meatball and Brown Bean Pie (see pages 96–7);* **opposite middle** *De Achterhoek Stockfish (pages 74–5);* **opposite right** *Poffertjes (see pages 122–3)*

This edition is published by Aquamarine
an imprint of Anness Publishing Ltd
www.aquamarinebooks.com
www.annesspublishing.com

© Anness Publishing Ltd 2022

If you like the images in this book and would like to investigate using them for publishing, promotions or advertising, please visit our website www.practicalpictures.com for more information.

Publisher: Joanna Lorenz
Senior Managing Editor: Conor Kilgallon
Project Editor: Emma Clegg
Designer: Simon Daley
Illustrator: Robert Highton
Photography: Debi Treloar
Food Stylist: Sunil Vijayakar
Prop Stylist: Helen Trent
Production Controller: Ben Worley

A CIP catalogue record for this book is available from the British Library.

PUBLISHER'S NOTE
Although the advice and information in this book are believed to be accurate and true at the time of going to press, neither the authors nor the publisher can accept any legal responsibility or liability for any errors or omissions that may have been made nor for any inaccuracies nor for any loss, harm or injury that comes about from following instructions or advice in this book.

COOK'S NOTES
Bracketed terms are intended for American readers.

For all recipes, quantities are given in both metric and imperial measures and, where appropriate, in standard cups and spoons. Follow one set of measures, but not a mixture, because they are not interchangeable.

Standard spoon and cup measures are level. 1 tsp = 5ml, 1 tbsp = 15ml, 1 cup = 250ml/8fl oz.

Australian standard tablespoons are 20ml. Australian readers should use 3 tsp in place of 1 tbsp for measuring small quantities of gelatine, flour, salt, etc.

American pints are 16fl oz/2 cups. American readers should use 20fl oz/2.5 cups in place of 1 pint when measuring liquids.

Electric oven temperatures in this book are for conventional ovens. When using a fan oven, the temperature will probably need to be reduced by about 10–20°C/20–40°F. Since ovens vary, you should check with your manufacturer's instruction book for guidance.

The nutritional analysis given for each recipe is calculated per portion (i.e. serving or item), unless otherwise stated. If the recipe gives a range, such as Serves 4–6, then the nutritional analysis will be for the smaller portion size, i.e. 6 servings. Measurements for sodium do not include salt added to taste.

Medium (US large) eggs are used unless otherwise stated in the text.

Contents

Geography of the Netherlands

The Netherlands, in north-western Europe, did not exist as a political entity until 1581 when the seven northern provinces founded a new republic, independent from Spain. Endless battles, treaties and alliances meant that the borders were constantly redrawn until they were finally settled in 1830, when the area split into the separate states of the Netherlands and Belgium. The Netherlands today consists of 12 provinces: Friesland, Groningen, Drenthe, Utrecht, Overijssel, Flevoland, Gelderland, Zeeland, North Holland, South Holland, North Brabant and Limburg.

Below left The dunes are a method of protecting the Low Countries against the North Sea at high tide, shown here by the "Slufter", a trench cut through the dunes on the island of Texel.

Below right The belts of canals around the centre of Amsterdam are a favourite target for sightseeing by boat. The canals were formerly used to supply the homes and storehouses of rich merchants.

The Netherlands is bordered by the North Sea to the north and west, Belgium to the south, and Germany to the east. It is a densely populated and geographically low-lying country, with its name translating as "low countries" or "low lands". The plural form is used because the Netherlands has its origin in the unification of the seven northern provinces. The Dutch themselves distinguish between the name of their country (Nederland, singular) and the kingdom (Nederlanden, plural). The region to the south and east consists mostly of plains and a few high ridges, whereas the western and northern region is lower and includes reclaimed land (polders) on the site of the Zuiderzee and the delta of the Rhine, Meuse, and Schelde rivers. Coastal areas are almost all below sea level and the land is protected by dunes and artificial dikes.

Controlling the water flows around the country has always been key to its safety and prosperity. As far back as the Middle Ages, peasants drained peat bogs to make them into fertile agricultural areas. The drainage canals created to achieve this also provided an excellent method of commercial transport. This, combined with broad rivers, such as the Rhine and Meuse which provided access to the remotest parts of Europe, led to rapid urban and commercial development. In the 17th century, Amsterdam was seen as the world's commercial centre. Rotterdam harbour is still one of the biggest in the world, and commerce, transportation and agriculture are still essential to the Dutch economy. Due to the low-lying nature of the lands, floods have occurred frequently throughout the country's history, and still pose a physical threat.

Because the country is bordered by the North Sea, the Dutch have always been excellent fishermen and international traders. The flat soil and the mild maritime climate, with cool summers and mild winters, made it ideal for agriculture and cattle-breeding. In fact, one-third of the world's dairy cattle are the familiar black-and-white Dutch Holstein Friesians. Pigs and chickens have also been a traditional source of protein and until recently were very intensively farmed.

As well as being a country of rich pastures for raising cattle and, therefore, a producer of high-quality dairy products and good beef and veal, the country cultivates a range of fruits and vegetables. The potato has been a Dutch staple for centuries and apples have been cultivated since at least the Middle Ages. Cereals, such as barley and rye, have played an important role in the development of Dutch cuisine, as well as in their world-famous brewing industry. Products grown under glass or in polytunnels include flowers, tomatoes, and more recently (bell) peppers. Flower bulbs such as tulips and daffodils are cultured behind the dunes, the sale of cut flowers and potted plants being a leading industry.

Above Large numbers of windmills were traditionally used for effective land drainage. While their task has now been taken over by pumping stations, working mills are still a common sight. Countless canals and ditches divide the Dutch polders into neat rectangles.

Above right The flatness of the country and the rich, mostly alluvial, soil made the Netherlands an ideal place for cattle breeding and agriculture. Cheese, vegetables and fruit are important export products.

Right Bulbous plants, especially tulips and daffodils, are grown primarily on the mixed soil of low fen and sand directly behind the dunes.

The development of Dutch cooking

Records tracing a nation's food heritage are rare, and the names of chefs and cooks in the past and the delicacies they invented have hardly ever been preserved. It was not until after the 1920s that daily life in the Netherlands became more carefully documented as a historical record. The following pages trace the essentials of the food preferences in the "land of milk and honey", as the Netherlands was called in the 17th century (the period now referred to as the *Gouden Eeuw*, or Golden Age), and how they related to the culture and events of the time.

Some ten to twelve thousand years ago, the area now called the Netherlands was a tundra stretching as far as England. Hunters from Hamburg and Ahrensburg roamed there, eating reindeer and fish. Archaeologists have discovered that the first great culinary revolution took place 7,000 years ago when the first Dutch farmers settled on the "Löss" grounds of Limburg, clay grounds highly suitable for agriculture. Their diet was oriented around sheep, cattle, goats and pigs and cultivated produce such as emmer wheat, peas, lentils, linseed and poppy seed. About 500 BC, the coastal areas of the middle (Holland) and the north (Friesland and Groningen) also became farmland. Archaeological finds prove that as early as about 150 BC cheese was being made in earthen moulds.

The Roman era

Roman cuisine was introduced around the beginning of the first century. At that time, Dutch was not a written language, so everything known about that period comes from the Romans, especially the historian Tacitus. In his book *Germania*, written in AD 98, he describes the tribes of the Batavians and Caninefates, or "rabbit catchers," who lived in those regions, "Their food is very simple; wild fruit, fresh venison, or coagulated milk. They banish hunger without formality, without curious dressing and curious fare." (Tr. Thomas Gordon.)

Not only did the Dutch derive the word *koken*, to cook, from the Romans, they also learned how to prepare food the Roman way. Roman cuisine had taken over the rich culinary heritage of the Greeks, who, in turn, had drawn significantly from the cuisine of Persia after the conquests of Alexander the Great. The Persians themselves had learned a lot from the Babylonians who inhabited what is now Iraq. Thus, the ultimate roots of modern European cuisines, including that of the Netherlands, lay in the Middle East.

The Middle Ages

In the period around AD 400, the climate of the Netherlands became colder and wetter, large areas of land were washed away and vast marshes were formed. This was when the Dutch started to reclaim land from the sea. Churches and monasteries, the centres of learning in the Middle Ages, also became the focus of culinary culture.

Records from monasteries and city archives, as well as medieval paintings and miniatures, provide information about how the rich ate. They were served a lot of game and poultry, including braised swans, peacocks or herons, displayed in their own feathers on gold or silver dishes. When Charles the Bold married Margaret of York in Brugge in 1468, 24 game dishes were served at the wedding feast,

Below Edam is a rotund cheese with a low fat content, a mild taste and a smooth texture. It was always sold in the market at Alkmaar, and, for the benefit of tourists, carts full of Edam still appear in the market square. It is said that the distinctive flavour of this cheese can be attributed to the rich grazing pastures of North Holland.

In 1588, Carel Baten's 1000-page *Medicine Book* was published, the popular second edition of which included a cookbook including many exotic ingredients not grown in northern Europe, such as lemons and oranges, and also some vegetables, such as spinach, stewed with wine, apples and sugar. Cauliflower and Savoy cabbage, just beginning to be imported from Italy, were served with ground ginger. The recipes have wide-ranging international influences, a large number from France, as well as Spain, Italy and Germany.

The cuisine of the wealthiest was extraordinarily exotic at the time. Oranges, lemons and grapes were imported from southern Europe, while foreign spices and daring combinations, such as carp with gingerbread sauce, were the height of fashion.

The importance of eating healthy foods such as fruit and vegetables was fully recognized in the Netherlands of the 16th century, although many were hard to get hold of and had prices that made them only accessible to the privileged classes. Paintings by Dutch artists such as Joachim Beuckelaer (1533–73), Jan Victors (1620–76) and Jan van Huysum (1682–1749) show an abundance of vegetables and fruit on the tables of the rich, commissioned to display the luxury of the owners' lifestyles.

Left Many small houses in the countryside, like this one in Brabant, have their own vegetable and fruit gardens. While men till the soil occasionally, this role is generally carried out by the lady of the house.

Below Numerous Dutch still lives, such as this one by Jan van Huysum (ca.1725), were intended to show off the opulence of their owners' lifestyles. The peaches and fresh grapes shown here did not grow easily in the Dutch climate.

accompanied by large "trees" made of glacé (candied) fruit, such as apples, pears and cherries. Two male and female dwarfs stood on the tables next to each dish holding fruit baskets. In the same period, the more common people ate simple stews, although there were periods of famine as a result of war or poor harvests, as in the disastrous years 1315–17.

The Middle Ages, dark for Europe, saw a period of brilliance in the Middle East, when science and the economy flourished. This period also saw the start of a green revolution that recommended the increased consumption of vegetables, in particular an emphasis on serving delicious, fresh salads at the start of a meal. This influence was clearly reflected in the cuisine of the Netherlands.

Foreign influences

In the early 15th century, the counts, dukes and bishops who had ruled the Low Countries in the Middle Ages had to come to terms with the growing influence of the Dukes of Burgundy, powerful princes of the French royal house of Valois. When Charles V, who was also Duke of Burgundy, became Holy Roman Emperor in 1530, French cultural influences, including culinary style and habits, became more evident throughout the Netherlands.

The Golden Age

Towards the end of the 16th century, a period of economic prosperity and cultural growth began in the Netherlands, now known as the Golden Age. During this period, the Dutch became a major economic power and colonies and trading posts were established worldwide, including the Dutch East Indies (Indonesia), Suriname in South America, Dutch Ceylon (Sri Lanka), the Netherlands Antilles in the Caribbean and South Africa. Remaining under the Dutch Empire until the fall of imperialism in the 20th century, the food culture of these colonies became well assimilated in the Netherlands, in particular with the use of South-east Asian herbs and spices, although rather than directly influencing Dutch traditions, they tended to be absorbed as authentic, specialist cuisines.

The Golden Age saw a dramatic change in society with the introduction of the oven, built in brick in the grand houses of rich merchants, especially those of the powerful East India Company. One-pot cooking became a thing of the past for such families because more dishes could be prepared at the same time.

During this period, vegetables, salads and fresh fruit became even more popular. The ultimate status symbol was a country estate and a generous size garden with flowers as well as all kinds of indigenous and foreign edible plants. Some believe that this emphasis on cultivation signified the shift towards a more rural lifestyle, while others see it more as an adjustment of dietary habits in light of new ideas about the science of digestion and healthy eating. Sugar was banished to

dessert, and fresh herbs and vegetables were preferred to dried spices and pulses. This preference must have been endorsed by the frequent outbreaks of scurvy, a disease caused by a deficiency of vitamin C, in sailors on the long sea voyages of the 16th and 17th centuries, which made doctors emphasize the importance of eating fruit and vegetables.

The influence of Calvinism

In the 17th-century republic in the Netherlands, to enjoy virtually anything was seen as suspect, even sinful. This way of thinking was built on a predominantly Calvinistic culture. The officially approved Reformed prayers said before and after a meal strongly emphasized strict moderation at the table and a preoccupation with the "bread" of the Word of God. The lawyer-poet Jacob Cats (1577–1660) endorsed this rejection of the pleasures of food and his influence further repressed the development of Dutch cookery, as these lines demonstrate: "Let gorging be enjoyed by those who live for gluttony ... The gullet is a wolf, and what people eat slips down in haste and is immediately forgotten." Wining and dining continued behind closed doors, seen as admissible, as long as you did not make a show of it to your neighbours.

Aristocratic tastes

Almost all provinces of the Netherlands published their own cookbooks in the 18th century. The recipes were mostly written by ladies who read them out loud to their maids. The authors were obviously passionate about their work, and often added the word *puik*, meaning excellent, at the end of their recipes.

While the lower classes in the country were poverty stricken, the well-to-do continued to enjoy French cuisine, using books written by French chefs, which

featured anchovy toasts, truffled minced (ground) veal and instructions for braising a whole suckling pig and serving it with a lemon in its mouth. The bestselling cookbook was *Alice the Perfect and Thrifty Kitchenmaid*, first published in 1803. Despite the adjective "thrifty", the recipes follow the previous century's rich cuisine, using lots of eggs, expensive butter and wine. It includes the first mashes and the combination of potatoes, vegetables and meat that are still the foundation of Dutch daily meals.

19th-century hardship

Industrialization dawned slowly in the Netherlands of the 19th century, in comparison to the rest of Europe, because of the country's reliance on water transport and wind power. This saw an undermining of its economic power by Great Britain's sea forces and the French army under Napoleon. This period also saw famine strike in the Netherlands, a period documented in Vincent van Gogh's (1853–90) sombre painting, *The Potato Eaters*, showing a peasant family, probably farmers or miners, gathered around the table to eat a humble meal of potatoes. During this period, soup was widely distributed by public kitchens.

Several domestic science schools were opened in the late 19th century, irreverently called Spinach Academies. Most of them produced rather dull, healthy recipes, or what passed for healthy at the time. They had a disastrous effect on Dutch cooking. Their cookbooks were intended to teach the poverty-stricken working class how to cook properly and frugally, but they were (and often still are) widely regarded as middle-of-the-road cuisine. However, the traditions of the true Dutch cuisine continued to make themselves felt at home, where mothers taught their daughters how to make their favourite dishes. This "secret cuisine" of the Netherlands is recorded in handwritten notebooks that now command steep prices.

Left *The Graaf Floris is a well-known pub situated on the Vismarkt in the centre of Utrecht. Often patronised by students, this venue breathes the easy-going atmosphere of an inexpensive Dutch restaurant.*

A new perspective

Two world wars left scars on the infrastructure and economic prosperity of the country. The years following World War II saw massive efforts to rebuild and increase prosperity. This period also shows a definite move away from the influence of Calvinism and an interest in new ways of preparing food. Cooking became democratic, men acknowledged their interest more openly, and cooks became famous chefs. In the Netherlands of today, this change of perspective is making itself felt as distinguished young chefs, such as Jonnie Boer, are developing Dutch cuisine around the world, inspired by regional produce and almost-forgotten local dishes.

The 1990s saw a revival of the "secret cuisine" of the Netherlands with restaurant-led campaigns and promotions of regional products. There is also an enthusiasm for seasonal ingredients. One chef, Albert Kooij, explains that, "You should see on the table in which environment you are eating and in which season." In cities, such as in Amsterdam on the Noordermarkt, products can now be bought directly from farmers.

Despite these developments, the cross-fertilization of culinary influences and the appeal of global food brands mean that European cuisine is less enriched by regional traditions, as palates have adapted to the influence of other cultures. This book aims to go back to the authentic roots of Dutch cooking, with recipes that emphasize the peculiar, the unique, and the characteristic, in the hope that the recipes will be cooked and enjoyed in appreciation of their tradition as well as offering, for many, a new taste experience.

Left *The Potato Eaters by Van Gogh (1853–90) expresses the sombre mood of the poor who often had nothing but potatoes to eat in the period when famine struck the Netherlands in the 19th century.*

Festivals and celebrations

Nowadays a huge number of holy days is celebrated in the Netherlands throughout the year, including those of various Christian denominations, and Buddhists, Hindus and Muslims. It is impossible to mention them all here, so this account is confined to the officially recognized festive days – not all of them religious celebrations – when almost everybody gets a day off to celebrate. These days are included if a special food or drink is traditionally associated with them.

New Year's Day

The year starts and ends with home-made *oliebollen* and *appelflappen*, which are these days usually accompanied by champagne or other sparkling wine. Some people prefer an old-fashioned mulled wine, called "bishop-wine", made by simmering red Bordeaux with a lemon decorated with cloves and sugar. Other New Year dishes include Hussar's Salad, Herring Salad and other small salads (*slaatjes*), which the Dutch share with their neighbours when setting off fireworks at midnight.

Carnival

Every spring, just before Ash Wednesday, a carnival is celebrated for three days. While now only remotely connected with the Catholic Church, those who have fasted during Lent still welcome the return to normal food. Cities and villages have their own carnival clubs, headed by an elected "prince". Floats parade the streets, special carnival hits are sung and beer is consumed in large quantities. Many people open their doors for guests who are treated to tubs full of soup and herring.

Palm Sunday

On the Sunday before Easter, the custom is for children to carry a palm cross (*palmpaasje*) decorated with ribbons, strings of dried fruit, and small bread figures in the shape of swans or cockerels, called *palmpasenbrood*.

Easter

During this Christian celebration, coloured eggs, symbols of new life at the beginning of spring, are seen everywhere, with sweet eggs consumed in large quantities. Beautifully decorated chocolate eggs are offered for sale by pâtissiers, together with chocolate hares (jack rabbits), chosen because of the fertility of the species. Bakers also sell *paasmannetjes*, Easter men, little bread men clasping a cooked egg in their arms, and the sugared *paaskrakelingen*, Easter cracknels, made from bread dough or puff pastry. The shape of these cracknels is thought to be a symbol of life and death, following the cycle of a seed sown in the ground, then the shoot growing above ground, then withering and, finally, "dying" for a short time.

Below left Carnival celebrations are celebrated all over the Netherlands, with most cities and villages organizing their own carnival over three days just before Ash Wednesday.

Below right Queen Beatrix celebrated Queen's Day on 30 April, the anniversary of her succession and of her mother's birthday. She abdicated in favour of her son, Willem-Alexander, in 2013 on that day. Large crowds typically gather to greet the monarch during the celebration.

Koningsdad

In the past, the birthday of the Dutch monarch was celebrated on the birthday itself, but nowadays, 27 April (or 26, to avoid a Sunday) is the celebration day. Early in the morning the national tricolour is flown, with an orange streamer symbolizing the House of Orange, the Dutch royal family. Bands march in the streets and almost every city and village organizes a fair. The royal family visits a different city or village every year, mingling freely with the crowds. People eat orange-coloured cakes and drink *oranjebitter*, an orange liqueur made specially for the occasion.

Halloween

This celebration on 31 October is now established in most parts of the Netherlands. Pumpkins are hollowed out with cut-outs for eyes, nose and mouth, and a light is placed inside to shine at night. The flesh can be used to make a delicious soup.

Saint Martin's Day

Celebrated on the Friday or Saturday preceding 11 November, children used to dress up and go from house to house with a candle in a hollowed fodder beet, singing special songs, whereupon they were rewarded with sweets (candy) or cake. Nowadays, children walk the streets with Chinese lanterns, mostly accompanied by adults. At home, a hearty Saint Martin's soup with a Dutch rusk awaits them.

Saint Nicholas

This saint is the Dutch equivalent of Santa Claus, a benevolent Christmas figure who distributes gifts on 5 December. During the preceding fortnight, children place small presents for the saint in their shoes each evening with some hay and a carrot for his horse.

The story of Saint Nicholas, or *Sinterklaas,* says that he travels to the Netherlands by steamer from his home in Spain. When he arrives, he stands there in his bishop's robes, surrounded by his servants, all called "Black Peter", armed with sacks full of sweets for all good children. These include chocolate letters, puff pastry filled with almond paste, marzipan, *taaitaai* – "chewy chewy" – and *speculaas,* an almond paste cake (see pages 144–5). On the evening of 5 December, the whole family gathers to receive presents. At the start of the evening, a Peter's black hand throws "pepper nuts", tiny balls, made from *speculaas*' dough, through the half-opened door into the room. This traditional Dutch feast now competes with the more modern Santa Claus who appears on 24 December, seen as a pagan intruder by most Dutch people.

Christmas

The whole country celebrates Christmas with enthusiasm, with the associated preparation of exquisite food. Traditional main dishes are beef roll, turkey and often game. *Kerstkransjes,* round biscuits (cookies) with a hole in them, are bought from the baker and are sprinkled with flaked (sliced) almonds and pearl sugar. Other baked treats are *kerstkransen,* puff pastry rings filled with almond paste and decorated with cherries, and the special currant bread filled with almond paste that was adopted from their German neighbours.

Above *Sinterklaas, or Saint Nicholas (280–342), is the patron saint of children in the Netherlands and Belgium. His arrival in mid-November attracts large Dutch crowds, both young and old. His story tells of him riding a white horse over the rooftops. Saint Nicholas' Eve, on 5 December, is when gifts are shared, each one with a poem from the saint.*

Left *Even in small villages, Sinterklaas is said to arrive by boat, from his home in Madrid, Spain. He is always accompanied by his Black Peters who distribute "pepper nuts" to the children.*

Dutch eating habits

Like all nations, the Dutch have their own eating habits, mealtimes, table manners and traditional cuisine, the main emphasis always being on the essential combination of vegetables, potatoes and meat. They are also fond of snacks and take frequent coffee breaks. Many visitors to the Netherlands judge the cuisine and food culture solely on the basis of its restaurants, which is misleading because they represent so many national cuisines. Below, the everyday traditions of the Dutch diet are described, from their preference for eating raw herring fresh from the catch, to popular types of street food.

Every national cuisine has its own characteristics and flavours. The reason that Dutch people like new-season herring or liquorice and pea soup is because they share a piece of national history. Similarly, the Dutch still eat smoked sausages, salted meat and dried fish, even though such methods of preservation are no longer a practical necessary.

Meals

Eating three meals a day has become a routine only over the last century. *Ontbijt*, or breakfast, is taken between 7 and 9 a.m. In its most luxurious form it consists of white, brown, rye, currant and sugar bread, rusks, spice cake, a boiled egg, cheese and

Below The Dutch love to eat raw matjes (fresh herring) by dangling the fish from their hand, preferably immediately after the fish have been brought to shore.

cold cuts. Jam and chocolate sprinkles are provided for the white and brown bread or rusks; sweet breads and spice cake are eaten just with butter. In addition, there will be orange and grapefruit juice, tea and coffee. However, at home, one slice of bread with jam or cheese usually precedes a hasty departure.

At about 10.30 in the morning, it is coffee time. This is mostly drunk with milk and sugar and accompanied with spice cake or cookies.

Middageten, lunch, usually resembles brunch. However, between midday and 2 in the afternoon, you can sit at a *koffietafel*, or coffee-table, if you have reason to celebrate or want to discuss business. The Brabant *koffietafel*, consisting of brandy with sugar, buns, sausage buns, brawn (head cheese) and everything you also get for a festive breakfast, is especially famous. More often, people have a few sandwiches and a glass of milk. The French custom of a heavier main meal at lunchtime is gaining ground.

Tea is served between 3 and 4 p.m. but it is not so elaborate as traditional English tea. Children usually have biscuits (cookies).

Avondeten, dinner, is served between 6 and 8 in the evening, although it is common to arrive at restaurants between 7 and 8. This is the main meal for most Dutch people and consists of soup or a salad, a main course and a dessert.

Food etiquette

The Rotterdam scholar, Desiderius Erasmus, wrote about table manners in 1530, when people still ate with their hands from a common dish. He advised against spitting, blowing your nose in your napkin, licking your fingers or drinking wine more than twice during the meal. While Erasmus's advice became a strict convention, the Dutch also like to break these rules. They eat with a knife and fork, but will say that nothing tastes as good as a piece of smoked sausage or a chunk of cheese eaten with your fingers.

The Dutch are hospitable and love to invite guests to a meal. However, as they like to be well prepared, they don't like uninvited guests. A birthday, however, means open house when visitors are welcomed throughout the day. Treats are sweet tarts and pies, coffee, tea, cookies, savoury snacks, after which the adults are offered a *borrel*, or drink. This convention is summed up in one word, dear to all the Dutch – *gezellig*, or cosy.

Eating out

Dutch families go to restaurants less frequently than other Europeans, but when they do go out, it is often to eat non-Dutch food, with more than 80 countries represented in the restaurants of Amsterdam. Such venues typically represent the cuisines of countries such as China, Indonesia, Suriname, Italy and Greece. Chinese restaurants are a perennial favourite, and most of them offer a mixture of Chinese and Indonesian dishes – Indonesia was a Dutch colony until 1949 and the Dutch remain fond of Indonesian food.

As well as restaurants, there are many cafés, serving both coffee and alcoholic drinks. Snacks, such as *bitterballen*, are also frequently available.

There are cafeterias, snack bars, with a choice of fast food, such as salads, chips (French fries), Indonesian-style *loempia*, *nasi* or *bami slice*, croquettes, "bear claws", sliced meatballs with onions in between, and *belegde broodjes*, filled soft buns. The best place to find these buns is a *broodjeswinkel*, which is a bun store, not a sandwich bar. At the famous Amsterdam Eetsalon van Dobben, they serve buns with incredibly indulgent fillings. It's also certainly worth trying *pekelvlees*, a typically Dutch kind of pastrami.

In numerous *pannenkoekenhuizen*, or pancake restaurants, all over the country, you can order inexpensive pancakes with a wide variety of fillings. The Dutch like to eat them with treacle, even if the filling is savoury, such as cheese and bacon. In a traditional pancake restaurant in Leiden the pancakes are served on enormous Delft blue plates that evoke the traditions of rural life in the Netherlands.

Street food

If there is a smell of freshly fried fish at the fish stall, the Dutch love to take their children with them to buy and eat *lekkerbekjes*, deep-fried breaded whiting, hake or pollack. Another favourite is *kibbelingen*, formerly made of breaded salted cod cheeks, but nowadays using pieces of cheaper white fish. The Dutch will eat these with their fingers, standing together at the stall before taking home smoked mackerel, herring, salmon, eel or whatever fresh seasonal fish is available. Alternatively, they may decide to eat a herring at the *haringkar*, herring cart, which specializes in fresh herring and pickles.

New exotic specialities from Taiwan, Vietnam and other parts of South-east Asia available in Dutch marketplaces have not yet supplanted the *stroopwafelbakkers*, bakers of caramel waffles and the *gebakkraam*, literally meaning "pastry booth", where you can buy *oliebollen* all year round, as well as thick Belgian waffles and Berliner *bollen*, "balls from Berlin", deep-fried puffs filled with vanilla pudding.

Above The canal crossing the centre of the city of Utrecht provides low-lying wharfs with storage cellars. Many of these areas are nowadays occupied by restaurants.

Left Poffertjes, small sweet pancakes, are prepared using a cast-iron or copper pan with shallow indentations.

Dutch ingredients

Many typical Dutch foodstuffs will be familiar to cooks in other parts of the world, because they are used almost universally. Other more exclusive Dutch products, such as some types of Dutch cheese, are widely exported to other countries. On the pages that follow, standard Dutch ingredients are listed briefly, whereas the more specific ingredients, such as herring or the potato, are described in greater detail.

Fish

In the past, fish tended to be less favoured as an ingredient than meat because it was seen to have an insufficient amount of calories to sustain the manual lifestyles of the working population. Nowadays, the Dutch recognize the extensive health benefits of a diet full of fish, and salmon (smoked, especially in salads, and fresh), mussels, eel, cod (from the northern seas) and plaice are favourites. The traditional Dutch way of preparing any fresh fish is either to fry them in butter or to poach them and serve with melted butter, carrots, green peas and potatoes.

The most popular fish is Dutch herring – tender and flavoursome, more raw herring is consumed in the Netherlands than any other fish. The Dutch still commemorate Willem Beukelszoon from Biervliet, credited with the invention of *haringkaken*, or herring gutting, in 1350. The process involves cutting the throat away, together with the gills and some of the guts. The pancreas is left and this, in combination with salt, produces enzymes that enhance the fermentation. Modern cooling and preservation techniques have made it possible to keep the tender yet firm texture of new-season herring much longer than before.

The Dutch adore *maatjes* herring, which is young, raw herring without any roe. For some 50 years, the first new-season herring have landed in the harbour of Scheveningen, close to The Hague. Then *Vlaggetjesdag*, or Flags' Day, celebrates the official start of the new herring season around late May or early June. The ships are bedecked with flags and everyone, including the Queen, samples the *maatjes* herring.

The Dutch do not eat all their herring raw. *Zure haring* is marinated, while rolmops are marinated and rolled around a gherkin. Sometimes herring is baked and then marinated or it may be cold-smoked. It may also be steamed or pan-fried.

Meat

The Dutch love meat that can be produced so easily and cheaply in their country's flat landscape. Pork has been the most popular meat since the 12th-century, showing how food preferences remain well-engrained. Fried thick rashers of unsmoked bacon with red beets and potatoes are a popular dish, as is cauliflower with fried pork sausages.

The next most popular meat is chicken, which was traditionally fried whole on Sundays, but is now more commonly sold jointed. Beef is another favourite, and this is mostly sold in steaks. These are fried in butter, stewed for a long time, and then typically eaten with vegetables and potatoes. There is an enormous variety of secondary meat products, one of the most memorable being *rookvlees*, a very thinly sliced smoked beef, which is delicious on a slice of white bread and butter.

Guelders smoked pork sausage is a distinctive and much-loved ingredient. The only province that could boast lots of oaks and birch trees, Guelders was the first to practise the smoking technique. Top-quality butchers still smoke their sausages over birch chips and each year a competition is held in the town of Arnhem for the two types of smoked sausage – fine and coarse.

Other popular meat products include meatballs, *blinde vink*, thin meat slices, and *balkenbrij*, which is like a meat pudding made of pig's leftovers.

Below from left Trout (here shown as smoked fillets) is found throughout the lakes and rivers of the Netherlands; marinated herring, in contrast to fresh herring, keeps its skin and is cured in a salt brine; Guelders smoked pork sausage is a favourite delicacy, and forms an essential component of the national potato mashes.

Cheese puffs
Kaassoesjes

To give your guests a special surprise, try making these elegant cheese puffs as a delicious savoury titbit – these were highly popular in the 1960s and still have an enthusiastic following. **Makes 50**

100g/3³/₄oz/scant ¹/₂ cup butter
250ml/8fl oz/1 cup water
150g/5oz/1¹/₄ cups plain
  (all-purpose) flour
4 eggs

150g/5oz/1¹/₄ cups grated extra-
  mature (sharp) Gouda cheese
freshly grated nutmeg
salt and ground black pepper

1 Preheat the oven to 220°C/425°F/Gas 7. Line two baking sheets with baking parchment.

2 Heat the butter, water and salt to taste in a small covered pan over a low heat until the butter has melted. Bring to the boil, remove from the heat and tip in all the flour immediately.

3 Return the pan to heat and cook, stirring constantly, until the mixture comes away from side of the pan and forms a ball.

4 Transfer the dough to a bowl and beat in the eggs, one at a time, with a hand-held mixer fitted with dough hooks. Continue beating until the dough is smooth and glossy. Then mix in the 50g/2oz/¹/₂ cup of the cheese and season with nutmeg, salt and pepper to taste.

5 Using two teaspoons, place 25 small mounds of the mixture on the prepared baking sheets, spacing them about 5cm/2in apart. Bake for about 20 minutes, until puffed up and light golden brown.

6 Remove from the oven and leave to cool. Cut the puffs open with scissors and fill with the remaining cheese using a teaspoon.

7 Just before serving, heat through in a hot oven for a few minutes. Cheese puffs freeze well. Reheat frozen in a preheated oven at 220°C/425°F/Gas 7 for 10 minutes before serving.

Per item Energy 43kcal/181kJ; Protein 1.6g; Carbohydrate 2.3g,
of which sugars 0.1g; Fat 3.1g, of which saturates 1.8g; Cholesterol 22mg;
Calcium 29mg; Fibre 0.1g; Sodium 40mg.

Dairy products

The Dutch diet is unthinkable without dairy products, which are commonly eaten throughout the day. Most people start the morning with a buttered slice of bread and cheese, drink milk with their lunch and end their dinner with yogurt, rice porridge, *vla* or one of the many varieties of milk dessert that are nowadays available in supermarkets. Most Dutch are experts in the various types of cheese produced in their country and these cheeses are not only distinguished by their place of origin but also by the various stages of ripening. Many Dutch buy their cheese directly from a farmhouse where it is produced according to age-old recipes.

Gouda is by no means the only cheese from the Netherlands, but it is one of the best known. A hard Gouda-like cheese has been made in Holland since at least the Middle Ages. Gouda is sold at four stages of ripening: young, ripe, mature (sharp) and extra-mature, when it has a texture that is similar to Parmesan. This cheese is exported, and will therefore be a familiar sight, all over the world. Having said this, while Gouda-style cheeses are available in other countries, they rarely match an authentic Dutch cheese. Other well-known Dutch cheese includes Edam, Leyden, which is made with cumin seeds, and Frisian cheese, which is flavoured with cumin and cloves. Goat's cheese is also now gaining a sizeable market in the Netherlands.

Below from left Friese nagelkaas, *a cheese flavoured with cumin and cloves, was created when spices were imported to the Netherlands in the 17th century; and extra-mature Gouda cheese (*overjarig*).

Vegetables

The Dutch are famous for their vegetable growing, and this is a tradition that goes right back to the 16th century. England imported their vegetables from that time onwards and Catherine of Aragon, England's Tudor queen, used to have supplies of lettuce sent to her from Holland by a special high-speed sailing boat.

Salads are very popular. Lettuce is sixth in the top-ten rating of vegetables, preceded by onion, tomato, carrot, cucumber, cauliflower and followed by chicory (Belgian endive), green beans, leek and bell peppers. In terms of preparation, salad is typically made with a French dressing. The standard way of serving cucumber is to slice it very thinly and combine it with a dressing of vinegar, pepper and salt. Bell pepper, which is a relative newcomer, is cooked in the same way as Mediterranean countries. Other vegetables tend to be briefly boiled in water.

The potato is essential to every meal in the Netherlands, and never an optional extra. So seriously is it potato taken that there is a special recipe for a luxury potato purée (see right), served to accompany a festive dish. Varieties of potato are always specified, even in supermarkets, because people have definite favourites for different cooking techniques. Every bag of potatoes, therefore, will typically list its cooking qualities.

Below from left
Fresh leeks; shelled marrowfat peas, a common feature of the traditional diet but now less widely used.

Potato purée
Puree

When serving a festive dish, such as game, this luxury purée is piped on the rim of a shallow oven plate. It also surrounds cooked and drained chicory, is rolled into slices of cooked ham, or is alternatively covered with a cheese sauce and baked. **Serves 4**

750g/1lb 10oz peeled
   floury potatoes, cut
   into quarters
1/2 tsp salt
1/2 tsp paprika

1/2 tsp nutmeg
1/2 tsp black pepper
2 egg yolks
knob (pat) of butter
milk

1 Preheat the oven to 220°C/425°F/Gas 7. Grease an ovenproof dish with butter or line a baking sheet with baking parchment.

2 Put the potatoes in a pan, add water to cover, bring to the boil and cook for about 15 minutes, or tender. Drain well.

3 While still warm, pass the potatoes through a potato ricer or alternatively mash with a hand-held electric mixer, but take care as a mixer can produce a purée that is too sticky.

4 Stir in salt, spices, yolks, butter and some milk if the purée seems too thick.

5 While still warm, pipe or spread the purée with a fork into the prepared dish. Alternatively, pipe rosettes on to the baking sheet lined with baking parchment.

6 Bake the purée in the oven for 20 minutes.

Per portion Energy 174kcal/732kJ; Protein 4.5g; Carbohydrate 28.4g, of which sugars 2.3g; Fat 5.4g, of which saturates 2.3g; Cholesterol 106mg; Calcium 24mg; Fibre 1.8g; Sodium 236mg.

The new potato season is welcomed, so much so that every year the Dutch seed potatoes Alpha and Santé are exported to Malta and then re-imported a few months later, just before the season of the delicious Opperdoezer Ronde, a handpicked yellow-fleshed potato from North Holland. To this day it is common for Dutch people to take a supply of potatoes in their cars when travelling in the rest of Europe, especially in France where the main meal is often accompanied by bread, rather than potatoes.

Older potatoes are not only made into everyday mashes, but are prepared as a festive purée (see recipe on previous page), a word that, in Dutch, is specially used for potato purée.

Fruit
In the Netherlands fruit is produced both in glasshouses and field orchards, and all fruit is hand-picked. Berries are combined with yogurt and custard, made into fruit salads or used as a filling for pancakes. Apples and pears are widely grown and are often-used ingredients in various Dutch recipes. Pears, melons and strawberries are favourites, but the apple is by far the most popular, with more than 15 species available, among them the Alkmene and Elstar.

Dutch apple sauce and apple pie are always made with an irregularly shaped apple, called Goudrenet in the Netherlands and known as Belle de Boskoop in other countries. Its texture is similar to a russet while the flavour is quite sharp. This ancient variety owes its name to medieval monks who grafted

apples onto other stems. The modern Goudrenet was developed in the village of Boskoop around 1853. It can be substituted with Granny Smith in the Apple Pie (see pages 148–9) or the Appelflappen recipes (see page 143), or with any good-quality cooking apple when making apple sauce.

Amsterdam onions
These are large pearl onions, which are marinated in vinegar with sugar and mustard seeds and coloured yellow with kurkuma, a mild spice used for colouring. They are available in all supermarkets, but the finest, made following the original recipe containing 12 different ingredients, are sold by a specialist in Amsterdam (see suppliers on page 158) who pickles them himself. Some 150 years ago, Izak de Leeuw, an Ashkenazi Jew from Eastern Europe, sold these pickles from a handcart in Amsterdam. The large, sweet and sour gherkins from Jewish cuisine called *zure bommen* "sour bombs" are also a national delicacy.

Bread
In a country where two bread meals are the rule (for breakfast and lunch), it is not surprising that a large range of bread is available. A Dutch loaf is eaten in buttered slices, called *boterhammen*. Nowadays, wholemeal wheat bread is more popular than white. But the healthiness of brown bread took a long time to be established, because the Dutch remained fond of the soft white bread that was distributed after World War II to the starving

Below from left
Goudrenet, a commonly used Dutch cooking apple; marinated Amsterdam onions; Dutch spice cake, which is eaten at breakfast and with coffee; and sliced rye-bread, which is sold in Dutch bakeries and supermarkets.

 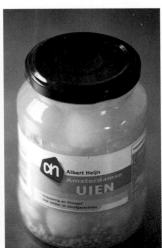  

population of the western provinces. Soft white or brown round and oblong rolls (which are bigger than hot dog rolls) often appear as part of a lavish breakfast, or are eaten while travelling. Currant bread and currant rolls are normally eaten at the weekend only. Recently acquired features to the nation's bread consumption are loaves covered and filled with seeds, and different forms of French-style bread.

There are two main types of *roggebrood*, or rye bread. Northern bread is very coarse and black, just like German pumpernickel, and is sweet and moist. The other type is the brownish, somewhat dry rye bread from Brabant and Limburg. Dark rye bread is great with new-season herring or cheese and the light type is wonderful with any kind of sausage, smoked ham or brawn (head cheese).

Koek, or spice cake, a kind of sweet soda bread, is the most frequently eaten treat at breakfast and with morning coffee. It is sold in countless variations: with orange peel, with nuts, with raisins or with candy. Nowadays it is advertised as a healthy product because it is made from rye flour and with no fat. The most famous is *Deventer koek*, named after the town, which has been famous for the cake since 1593.

Drinks

The Roman writer Tacitus mentioned in his description of the Low Countries that people drank beer and liked it so much that you could conquer them simply by serving it to them. Beer is still a favourite Dutch drink. It is also taken with meals, although wine – which was formerly a privilege of the higher classes – is now commonplace. As an aperitif, spirits are served, such as Jenever and brandy. Other popular drinks are white wine, brandied raisins or apricots (see right), redcurrant gin or advocaat (brandy with egg yolks and sugar).

Dutch gin, or Jenever, got its name from the juniper berries which give this its characteristic flavour. Also called *Corenwijn*, or grain-wine, this is a top-class Dutch gin distilled from barley, rye and, nowadays, maize (corn). In contrast to other, lesser-quality Dutch gins, it is made solely from cereals. The juniper berries are added during the fourth and final phase of distilling. This drink is matured in oak barrels for at least two years. It is still sold in earthenware bottles, in the same way as it would have been in the Middle Ages. It is best served straight from the freezer and is excellent eaten with new-season herring.

Country lads and girls
Boerenjongens en- meisjes

These "drinks", which are ladled from a small glass are a real Dutch speciality. The "lads", the brandied raisins, were a treat at wedding parties, especially in the north of the country. The "girls" are brandied dried apricots. Today both are also eaten spooned over ice cream and moulded puddings. You can buy them ready-made or make your own. **Serves 15**

250ml/8 fl oz/1 cup water
1 cinnamon stick (for the lads)
   or thinly pared rind of ½ lemon
   (for the girls)
100g/3¾oz/generous ½ cup sugar

250g/9oz/generous 1¾ cups
   sultanas (golden raisins) or
   halved dried apricots
500ml/17fl oz/generous 2 cups
   Dutch brandy

1 Put the water, sugar and cinnamon or lemon rind in a pan and bring to the boil, stirring until the sugar has dissolved.

2 Add the washed fruit and simmer for 10 minutes.

3 Transfer the mixture into a sterilized 750ml/1¼-pint/3-cup preserving jar. Leave to cool, then chill 48 hours.

4 Add the brandy, stir well and seal the jar. Store in a cool dark place for at least 6 weeks before serving. Serve in small wide stemmed glasses with a tiny silver spoon. Once opened, store in the refrigerator.

Per portion Energy 146kcal/614kJ; Protein 0.5g; Carbohydrate 18.5g, of which sugars 18.5g; Fat 0.1g, of which saturates 0g; Cholesterol 0mg; Calcium 14mg; Fibre 0.3g; Sodium 4mg.

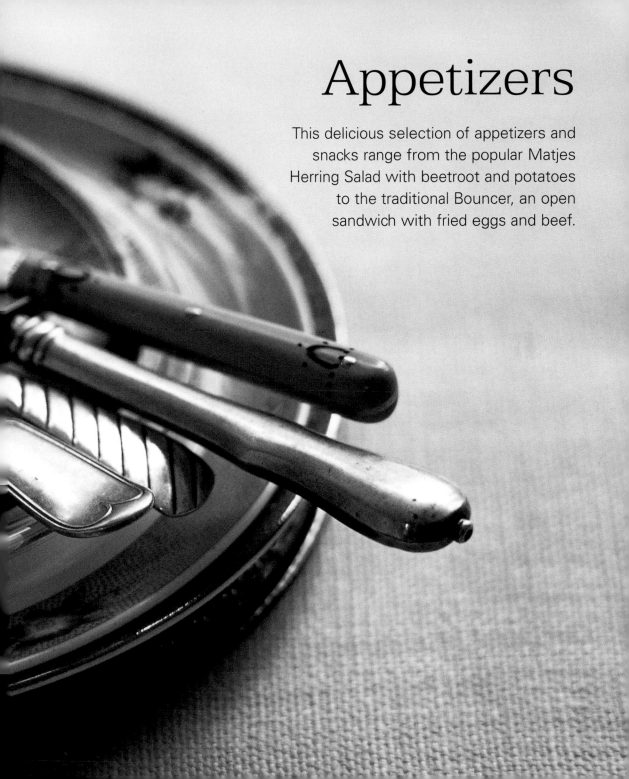

Appetizers

This delicious selection of appetizers and snacks range from the popular Matjes Herring Salad with beetroot and potatoes to the traditional Bouncer, an open sandwich with fried eggs and beef.

Snacks, sandwiches and salads

"At the start of the meal you shall eat something small and light … soft-boiled eggs in a salad of lettuce with herbs, vinegar and oil". This advice from a 16th-century Dutch cookbook by Doctor Gheeraert Vorselman is accompanied by recommendations for salads with lettuce, borage, mint, parsley, wild marjoram, fennel, fennel flowers, chervil, sorrel and other fragrant herbs dressed with vinegar and oil, or of young purslane leaves with chopped onion dressed with a pepper and cinnamon vinaigrette. This type of salad can still be found in contemporary Dutch restaurants, proof of the historical emphasis placed on fresh herbs and vegetables. The custom of starting a meal with a salad was, however, very much a tradition of the privileged classes, and it was only in the 1950s that salads started to appear more widely as an everday appetizer.

Dutch people used to have meals based on bread twice a day, for breakfast and lunch. Lunch included *slaatjes*, or small salads, and warme *hapjes*, or warm snacks. The snacks stem from pre-dinner drinks, or *'t borreluurtje*, served at 5 p.m. with assorted appetizers, which include deep-fried croquettes, cheese cubes and slices of what has since become a rather unpopular liver sausage (liverwurst). For a long time such luxuries were too expensive for most people, or were saved for very special occasions, but nowadays they are widely available.

The most popular drinks served with these snacks are still the traditional Jenever, a Dutch gin distilled from wheat, beer for men, white wine for women, or the traditional sweet Jenever with red berries (*bessenjenever*), or brandy with sugar (*brandewijn met suiker*). Many Dutch pubs have a special *borreltafel*, or happy hour table, for regular visitors.

As well as these long-established appetizers, the Dutch also developed more sophisticated dishes that have now become classics and appear regularly on every table. It is from these that the selection in this chapter was made.

8 eggs
65g/2½oz/5 tbsp butter
65g/2½oz/9 tbsp plain (all-purpose) flour
30ml/2 tbsp ready-made brown
    mustard, such as Dijon
salt and ground black pepper
celery leaves, to garnish
toast and butter, to serve

Kampen sturgeon
Kamper steur

This famous dish is from Kampen, a city in the eastern Netherlands on the river IJssel. The story goes that the city council, preparing for a visit from the Prince of Liège, ordered a local fisherman to catch a fine sturgeon. When the prince did not show up, they released the fish back into the river with a little bell around its neck so they could trace it when it was needed. Naturally when the Prince did arrive, the ruse failed and so the citizens of Kampen created this improvised "sturgeon" recipe – with no sturgeon.

1 Boil the eggs in a small pan of water for 10 minutes.

2 Meanwhile, melt the butter in another small pan over a low heat. Stir in the flour and cook, stirring constantly, for 2 minutes, then gradually stir in 600ml/1 pint/2½ cups water. Season with salt and pepper and simmer, stirring frequently, for 5 minutes.

3 Using a slotted spoon, remove the eggs from the pan, plunge into cold water and shell them. Cut each egg in half lengthways.

4 Remove the sauce from the heat, whisk in the mustard and pour it on to a warm flat serving plate.

5 Arrange the eggs, cut side up, on the sauce, garnish with celery leaves and serve with warm toast and butter.

Variation
Finely chop boiled eggs, keeping the whites and yolks apart. Arrange in rows, with a row of finely chopped celery leaves. Cover with a fried fillet of fish. Ladle the sauce over it.

Per portion Energy 325kcal/1350kJ; Protein 14.7g; Carbohydrate 13.5g, of which sugars 0.9g; Fat 24.3g, of which saturates 11g; Cholesterol 412mg; Calcium 88mg; Fibre 0.5g; Sodium 453mg.

Samphire with brown prawns
Zeeuwse zeekraal

Salicornia europea or marsh samphire, also known as glasswort, grows naturally on the salt marshes of the province of Zeeland in the far south-west of the Netherlands. Before the 20th century it was regarded as food fit only for poor people and sheep, but it is now a common sight in fashionable restaurants. The odd little stems, which look a little like a cactus, taste best fried quickly in butter, giving them a crunchy bite. The natural salty taste combines superbly with the small brown prawns or "crangon crangon" from the North Sea, with prawns from Stellendam fisherman's harbour a local favourite.

1 First of all wash the samphire thoroughly in cold water, and carefully remove any woody parts, along with pieces of shell and seaweed.

2 Melt the butter in a large frying pan. Add the spring onions and cook them over a low heat, stirring occasionally, for 3–5 minutes, until softened.

3 Add the samphire to the pan and cook, stirring constantly, for 1–2 minutes, until it is just beginning to wilt.

4 Add the prawn, increase the heat to medium, and cook quickly until just warmed through. Pour in the white wine, toss lightly and serve immediately with slices of bread.

Variations
• In Zeeland, the salty vegetable samphire, which is in season from mid-May to mid-September, is also eaten fresh as a salad with dressing. Always use very young plants as the stems become woody with age.
• Instead of samphire, use sea aster, in Zeeland called *lamsoor* (lamb's ear).

Serves 2

250g/9oz marsh samphire
40g/1½oz/3 tbsp butter
2 spring onions (scallions),
    coarsely chopped
100g/3¾oz/scant 1 cup cooked
    peeled brown prawns (shrimp)
    or other small prawns
15ml/1 tbsp white wine
white bread slices, to serve

Cook's tip
In Zeeland, where this dish originates, a local white wine would be used in the recipe, because early-ripening grape varieties now thrive well there. A good alternative is a Pinot Blanc. Serve the dish with a glass of the same wine.

Per portion Energy 190kcal/785kJ; Protein 2.2g; Carbohydrate 6.7g, of which sugars 6.6g; Fat 16.8g, of which saturates 10.5g; Cholesterol 44mg; Calcium 70mg; Fibre 2.8g; Sodium 132mg.

Herring salad
Haringsla

Serves 4

1 lettuce, finely shredded
1 shallot, finely chopped
15ml/1 tbsp chopped fresh dill
15ml/1 tbsp vegetable oil
15ml/1 tbsp white wine vinegar
2 apples
2 cooked beetroots (beet)
2 boiled potatoes (optional)
15ml/1 tbsp cocktail onions
15ml/1 tbsp coarsely chopped
    gherkins, plus 30ml/2 tbsp of
    the vinegar from the jar
2–4 hard-boiled eggs
4 *matjes* herrings, with skin and
    backbones removed
salt and ground black pepper
chopped fresh chives, to garnish

Cook's tip
This salad is accompanied perfectly
by a small glass of Dutch gin.

Per portion Energy 315kcal/1323kJ; Protein 21.4g;
Carbohydrate 19.5g, of which sugars 18.8g; Fat 17g,
of which saturates 1.2g; Cholesterol 137mg;
Calcium 58mg; Fibre 2.3g; Sodium 901mg.

The Dutch love *matjes* herring, a special kind of tender herring that is
produced by gutting and salting the fish at sea immediately after they
have been caught. According to legend, the process was invented in the
14th century, but ancient documents prove that the technique was used
much earlier. In any case the herring favoured by the one and only Dutch
Pope, Adrianus VI (1459–1523), must have been of this type. You can
order this salad in most Dutch restaurants. The sweet-and-sour taste
of the onions and gherkins shows the culinary influence of Jewish
immigrants from Eastern Europe.

1 Mix together the lettuce, shallot, dill, oil
and vinegar in a bowl and season with salt
and pepper. Spread out on a flat platter.

2 Peel, core and dice the apples, then
peel and dice the beetroots (beet) and
potatoes, if using.

3 Mix together the apples, beetroots,
potatoes, if using, cocktail onions,
gherkins and vinegar from the jar in
another bowl. Then spoon the mixture
into the middle of the platter.

4 Mash the eggs with a fork. Make a border
of mashed egg around the platter. Garnish
with the chives.

5 Cut off and discard the tails of the
herrings and halve the fish. Curl the halved
fish over the middle of the dish and serve.

Variations
• Try eating these herrings like the Dutch –
take one by the tail, swing it through a bowl
of finely chopped, raw onions, look upwards
and let it slowly slide down your throat.
• Small herring titbits, sprinkled with raw
onion, are often served at parties on a
buttered round of dark rye bread, held
together with a cocktail stick (tooth pick)
decorated with a small Dutch paper flag.

Serves 4

300g/11oz smoked trout, cut into strips
150g/5oz lamb's lettuce
60ml/4 tbsp cress
2 radishes, sliced
30ml/2 tbsp very finely chopped
   fresh parsley
50g/2oz/½ cup cooked brown prawns
   (shrimp) or other small prawns
8 canned anchovy fillets, drained
15ml/1 tbsp grated horseradish
30ml/2 tbsp mayonnaise
salt and ground black pepper
lemon wedges, to garnish
toasted white bread and butter, to serve

Smoked fish and horseradish sauce
Gerookte vis met mierikswortel

This combination of cold horseradish sauce and smoked fish has been a Dutch classic since 1795. Smoked eel has always been the most popular choice for this dish, but it is now less easily available because it is endangered, so you can substitute the eel with any other smoked fish.

1 Place the smoked trout in a small dish, add water to cover and soak for 30 minutes. Drain and pat dry with kitchen paper.

2 Divide the lamb's lettuce among four plates. Arrange the cress around the edges of the plates and add the radishes. Place the trout strips in the lamb's lettuce and surround with a ring of parsley and a ring of prawns.

3 Top each plate with two anchovy fillets and garnish with lemon wedges.

4 Mix together the horseradish and mayonnaise in a bowl and season to taste with salt and pepper.

5 Serve the smoked fish with the horseradish sauce and with toast and butter.

Per portion Energy 134kcal/561kJ; Protein 19.5g; Carbohydrate 3.1g, of which sugars 2.7g; Fat 4.9g, of which saturates 0.3g; Cholesterol 30mg; Calcium 89mg; Fibre 1.4g; Sodium 413mg.

Terrine of smoked Limburg trout
Terrine van gerookte Limburgse forel

Limburg is a narrow strip of land along the river Meuse at a crossroads between France, Germany, the Netherlands and Belgium. Far removed from the influence of the capital's politicians, the city of Maastricht was an ideal place to establish a powerful bishopric and it was the Catholic clergy that determined the quality of Limburg's cuisine. This recipe, which evolved from this tradition, is a special gift from Remy Mooren, the chef at Castle Vaalsbroek in Vaals, east of Maastricht who calls it "a parish priest's delight".

1 Cook the carrot in a pan of boiling water for 10 minutes, until softened. Drain and refresh under cold running water. Line a non-stick, 6cm/2½in-deep rectangular cake tin (pan) with the slices of carrot.

2 Place the gelatine in a small bowl of cold water and leave to soak for 5 minutes, until softened. Meanwhile, bring the cream just to the boil in a small pan, then remove from the heat. Squeeze out the gelatine and dissolve it in the cream. Stir in the dill and season generously with salt and pepper.

3 Pour a layer of cream into the cake tin, place a trout fillet on top and cover with another layer of cream. Continue making layers until all the cream and fish have been used up. Chill the terrine in the refrigerator for 8 hours or overnight.

4 About 30 minutes before you are ready to serve, turn out the terrine and cut it into slices. Arrange the slices on a serving plate and leave to come to room temperature. Garnish with lettuce and tomato slices and serve with toast.

Makes 9 slices

1 large carrot, thinly sliced
15g/½oz gelatine leaves
500ml/17fl oz/generous 2 cups
   double (heavy) cream
30ml/2 tbsp finely chopped fresh dill
5 smoked trout fillets
salt and ground white pepper
oakleaf or frisée lettuce, toasted white
   bread and tomato slices, to serve

Cook's tip
A Müller-Thurgau wine from Maastricht's well-known vineyard Apostelhoeve is a good accompaniment to this dish.

Per slice Energy 348kcal/1437kJ; Protein 13.2g; Carbohydrate 1.9g, of which sugars 1.8g; Fat 32g, of which saturates 18.6g; Cholesterol 76mg; Calcium 38mg; Fibre 0.3g; Sodium 47mg.

Stone pudding
Steenpudding

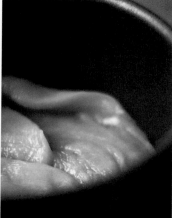

Serves 8

butter, for greasing
500g/1¼lb skinless chicken breast fillets
500g1¼lb minced (ground) chicken
30ml/2 tbsp breadcrumbs
50g/2oz onion, very finely chopped
15ml/1 tbsp finely chopped fresh parsley
15ml/1 tsp *rommelkruid* or mild paprika
salt and ground white pepper
lemon slices, to garnish
gherkins and pickled onions, to serve

Cook's tips
Traditionally, the weight used to compress
the mould is a foil-wrapped stone,
weighing about 1.6kg/3½lb. Ideally the
shape of the stone should approximate
that of the charlotte mould to evenly
distribute its pressure.

Per portion Energy 154kcal/653kJ; Protein 30.9g;
Carbohydrate 4.1g, of which sugars 0.5g; Fat 1.7g,
of which saturates 0.4g; Cholesterol 88mg;
Calcium 20mg; Fibre 0.3g; Sodium 105mg.

The typically Dutch flavour of this dish comes from an ingredient called
rommelkruid, meaning "jumble herbs". This used to be made with a rather
unhealthy mixture of spices and "Spanish red", an iron residue used to
enhance the colour. Today it gets a natural red colour from wood extracts.
This kind of *rommelkruid* is still used for Dutch gingerbread as well as for
making sausages. Mild paprika is a satisfactory substitute.

1 Grease a 1.2-litre/2-pint/5-cup charlotte
mould with butter.

2 Thinly slice the chicken fillets horizontally
with a sharp knife. Season and divide the
slices into four portions.

3 Mix together the minced chicken,
breadcrumbs, onion and parsley in a bowl
and stir in 5ml/1 tsp salt and pepper. Divide
the mixture into three portions.

4 Make a layer of the first portion of chicken
slices in the prepared mould and top with a
layer of one portion of the minced chicken
mixture. Carefully sprinkle with 5ml/1 tsp of
the *rommelkruid* or paprika, without letting it
stick to the sides of the mould.

5 Make layers until all the chicken has been
used, ending with a layer of chicken slices.

6 Cover the mould with a round of baking
parchment, one that reaches 2cm/¾in below
the rim, and tie it in place with kitchen
string. Press down firmly on the mould and
place a saucer on top. Place a weight on top
of the saucer.

7 Place the mould in a wide pan and add
boiling water to reach about three-quarters
of the way up the side. Cover and simmer
gently for 3 hours.

8 Remove the mould from the pan and
leave to cool for 12 hours.

9 Briefly dip the base of the mould in hot
water, then invert on to a plate. Garnish with
lemon slices and serve with pickles.

Variation
Use veal instead of chicken.

Bouncer
Uitsmijter

This open sandwich with eggs and beef is a traditional Dutch bar food. The derivation of its name could be because the eggs need to be removed from the pan very quickly, or because it was the last dish any guests could have before they were "bounced", or asked to leave the bar at closing time. It is seen as a typically Dutch dish, a meal that has been described as good "blotting paper" to soak up large amounts of beer and Dutch gin. It is certainly a favourite among social drinkers wanting a solid, filling meal.

1 Spread butter on one side of each slice of bread, then place on a serving plate and cover with the meat of your choice.

2 Arrange the lettuce leaves beside the bread. Cut the gherkin lengthways into several slices, leaving it attached at the top, and then spread out into a fan and place on top of the lettuce with the tomato quarters.

3 Melt the butter in a frying pan. When it is foamy but not brown, slide the eggs into the pan, keeping the yolks intact. Cook over a low heat until the whites are just set but the yolks are still runny. This is the classic way to cook *spiegelei*, or fried eggs.

4 Using a slotted fish slice or metal spatula, transfer the eggs to the bread. Sprinkle with the parsley, season with salt and pepper to taste and serve immediately.

Variations

• Cooked veal slices, minced (ground) veal and prawns (shrimp) may be substituted for the boiled ham or roast beef.
• The slices of bread may be fried in butter on both sides until golden before they are topped with the meat. Serve with mustard.
• If you prefer your eggs with crispy brown edges, cook them over a slightly higher heat.
• For a vegetarian bouncer, use slices of young or old Gouda cheese.

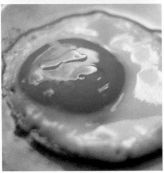

Serves 1

25g/1oz/2 tbsp butter, plus extra
   for spreading
2 slices white bread
4 slices boiled ham or roast beef
2–3 lettuce leaves
1 gherkin
1 tomato, quartered
2 eggs
15ml/1 tbsp chopped fresh parsley
salt and ground black pepper

Per portion Energy 593kcal/2481kJ; Protein 37g; Carbohydrate 31.8g, of which sugars 6.5g; Fat 36.6g, of which saturates 17.4g; Cholesterol 492mg; Calcium 173mg; Fibre 2.8g; Sodium 1787mg.

Serves 6

1 lettuce, coarse outer leaves removed
600g/1lb 6oz boiled potatoes
about 45ml/3 tbsp vegetable oil
about 45ml/3 tbsp white wine vinegar
5ml/1 tsp ready-made mustard
1 tart apple
4 gherkins, chopped
60ml/4 tbsp cocktail onions, chopped
1 cooked beetroot (beet),
    peeled and diced
300g/11oz cold cooked veal or
    beef, diced
2 hard-boiled eggs, finely chopped
150–250ml/5–8fl oz/⅔–1 cup mayonnaise
salt and ground black pepper
15ml/1 tbsp chopped fresh
    parsley, to garnish

Per portion Energy 425kcal/1768kJ; Protein 16.3g;
Carbohydrate 20.5g, of which sugars 5.2g; Fat
31.5g, of which saturates 6.1g; Cholesterol 111mg;
Calcium 39mg; Fibre 2g; Sodium 217mg.

Hussar's salad
Huzarensalade

This is a traditional New Year's Eve dish, which is served around midnight once the new year has arrived, but the Dutch also like to serve this salad on other festive occasions. The name is said to derive from the hussars, who were once stationed all over the Netherlands, and were generally underfed in their barracks. In desperation, they courted the kitchen maids of wealthy families, who fed them cold leftovers from their masters' kitchens.

1 Wash the lettuce leaves, line a shallow dish with them and set aside.

2 Mash the potatoes with the oil, vinegar and mustard in a bowl until smooth and season with and salt and pepper. You may need to add a little more oil and vinegar.

3 Peel and dice the apple. Set aside 15ml/ 1 tbsp each of the gherkins, onions and beetroot for the garnish.

4 Carefully mix the remainder with the mashed potato, then stir in the apple, meat and eggs.

5 Make a mountain of this mixture over the lettuce leaves, and then cover with a thick coating of mayonnaise.

6 Garnish with the reserved beetroot, gherkins and onions and sprinkle with the parsley before serving.

Variations
• The modern trend is to dice the potatoes in this dish rather than mash them. This is certainly tastier, but is more time-consuming.
• Peas and carrots make good additions to the salad.

Brabant brawn
Kipkap

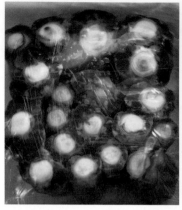

Serves 9

1.2kg/2½lb oxtail, cut into pieces
2 carrots, scraped
1 onion, halved
2 cloves
bouquet garni, made from 1 thyme
    sprig, 1 rosemary sprig, 2 parsley
    sprigs and tied with celery
200ml/7fl oz/scant 1 cup red wine
30ml/2 tbsp red wine vinegar
10g/¼oz gelatine leaves
vegetable oil, for greasing
15ml/1 tbsp chopped fresh parsley
15ml/1 tbsp chopped fresh chives
salt and ground black pepper

Cook's tips
• If you do not have a pressure cooker, use
a flameproof casserole or large pan with a
lid and simmer the meat for about
4 hours, until the meat is tender.
• You may need to strain the stock twice
as it has to be clear.

Per portion Energy 163kcal/683kJ; Protein 16.68g;
Carbohydrate 2.36g, of which sugars 2.1g; Fat
8.12g, of which saturates 0.1g; Cholesterol 0mg;
Calcium 18.7mg; Fibre 0.7g; Sodium 104mg.

In the Netherlands, brawn (head cheese) is a terrine made with meat from
a pig's head, and is traditionally combined with other leftover pieces of
fresh pork, such as the gelatinous trotters. Nowadays, the Dutch word for
this recipe, *kipkap,* means minced meat. This recipe uses oxtail to prepare
the stock that becomes the crystal clear brawn which is typical of Brabant,
in the south. Brawn is usually eaten cold as a luncheon meat.

1 Cook the oxtail, in batches, in an open
pressure cooker, without any added fat.
Cook over a low heat for 5–10 minutes on
each side until evenly browned.

2 Return the meat to the pressure cooker,
add the carrots, onion, cloves, bouquet garni,
wine, vinegar and 2.5ml/½ tsp salt and pour in
100ml/3½fl oz/scant ½ cup water. Cover and
bring to high pressure, then cook for 2 hours.

3 Remove the meat from the pan with a
slotted spoon and reserve the stock. Place
the cooked oxtail in a sieve (strainer) and
rinse under cold water, then drain and cool.
Remove the meat from the bones and cut
into neat pieces, discarding any sinews. Chill
for several hours in the refrigerator.

4 Ladle the stock through a strainer lined
with dampened muslin (cheesecloth) into a
bowl. Add water to make up 500ml/17fl oz/
generous 2 cups, if necessary.

5 Place the gelatine in a bowl of water and
soak for 5 minutes. Bring 50ml/2fl oz/¼ cup of
stock to the boil, then remove from the heat.
Squeeze out the gelatine and dissolve it in the
stock. Stir into the rest of the stock, then
taste and season if necessary. Chill until set.

6 Brush a 1-litre/1¾-pint/4-cup mould with
oil and ladle a thin layer of half-set stock
into it. Sprinkle the stock with half the
parsley and chives and chill until fully set.

7 Reserve 150ml/¼ pint/⅔ cup of the stock
and mix the rest with the meat. Ladle the
meat mixture into the mould and sprinkle
with the remaining herbs. Stand the
reserved stock in hot water for a few
seconds until it is liquid, then gently ladle
the stock over the herbs. Chill in the
refrigerator until set.

8 Turn out the dish, cut into thick slices with
a sharp knife and serve.

Meat croquettes
Vleeskroketten

Makes 8

200g/7oz lean veal, cut into pieces
2.5ml/½ tsp salt
40g/1½oz/3 tbsp margarine
1 onion, cut into wedges
1 carrot, halved
1 fresh parsley sprig
1 fresh thyme sprig
1 bay leaf
1 mace blade
6 black peppercorns
250ml/8fl oz/1 cup hot water
25g/1oz/¼ cup plain (all-purpose) flour
1 egg yolk
5ml/1 tsp very finely chopped fresh parsley
few drops of lemon juice
vegetable oil for deep-frying
salt and ground black pepper

For the coating

115g/4oz/2 cups fine breadcrumbs
2 eggs
10ml/2 tsp olive oil

For the garnish

ready-made mustard
deep-fried parsley sprigs

Per item Energy 247kcal/1028kJ; Protein 9.3g;
Carbohydrate 14.3g, of which sugars 1g; Fat 17.4g,
of which saturates 1.7g; Cholesterol 94mg;
Calcium 41mg; Fibre 0.6g; Sodium 344mg.

Dutch restaurants and pubs serve croquettes with two slices of bread and a sprig of deep-fried parsley. Most meat croquettes are now ready-made, the best using gelatinous veal. For a typical Amsterdam croquette, a good-quality, light margarine should be used instead of butter. This is to cater for Jews, who cannot mix meat and dairy.

1 Season the veal with the salt. Melt 10g/¼oz/1½ tsp of the margarine, add the veal and cook over a medium heat for about 5 minutes, until evenly browned. Add the onion, carrot, parsley, thyme, bay leaf, mace, peppercorns and hot water, bring to the boil, then lower the heat, cover and simmer for 1–2 hours, until the meat is tender. Remove the veal with a slotted spoon and dice it finely. Strain the stock into a bowl and reserve 200ml/7fl oz/scant 1 cup.

2 Melt the remaining margarine in a pan over a low heat, without allowing it to colour. Stir in the flour and cook for 2 minutes, then stir in the reserved stock. Cook until thickened.

3 Beat the egg yolk with a small ladleful of the sauce in a bowl, then stir the mixture into the pan. Stir constantly for a few seconds until thickened not allowing the mixture to boil. Remove from the heat.

4 Stir the meat into the sauce, season and stir in the parsley and lemon juice. Spread evenly over a plate, leave to cool and chill for at least 2 hours.

5 Divide the meat mixture into eight portions and shape into cylindrical croquettes with two spoons. Spread out the breadcrumbs in a shallow dish. Beat the eggs with the olive oil in another shallow dish and season.

6 Roll the croquettes in the breadcrumbs, dip them in the beaten egg mixture and roll them in the breadcrumbs again. Flatten the ends. Put the croquettes on a plate and chill in the refrigerator until you are ready to cook them.

7 Heat the vegetable oil in a deep-fryer or pan to 180°C/350°F or until a cube of day-old bread browns in 30 seconds. Deep-fry the croquettes in two batches for 5–6 minutes, until chestnut brown. Remove with a slotted spoon and drain on kitchen paper. Serve with mustard and deep-fried parsley.

Variations
Form the chilled meat mixture into walnut-size balls to make *bitterballen*, or "bitter balls". These are part of the *bittergarnituur*, or canapés, served with drinks, mostly iced Dutch gin, around 5 p.m. These include cubes of cheese, sliced sausage and gherkins.

Soups

Dutch soups are inspired by the rustic tradition of warming, wholesome meals and by the lighter, sophisticated creations of the Dutch aristocracy – those included here range from Broad Bean Soup from De Achterhoek and Queen's Soup, an adaptation of a French recipe.

Pottage and bouillon

Making soup is an ancient tradition that can be traced back to the introduction of the earthen cooking pot at the end of the Stone Age, which enabled bones and otherwise useless scraps to be turned into nourishing dishes. Adding herbs, vegetables and fruit to the brew in the pot has created endless new possibilities for creative cooks, and has helped to define national dishes and flavours in every part of the world. Perhaps most importantly of all, soup is a very inclusive social dish – just adding a little extra water gives an extra portion for an unexpected guest.

One-pot cooking was the only way of preparing food on a single open fire or kitchen range. Even after the introduction of the stove, pottage, or *pottaedje*, as thick soups were called, remained the common food of most families. In the countryside, in areas such as Brabant and De Achterhoek, it was only in the 1960s that the stove became a more common feature of the household kitchen. As a result, such regions have established some of the most flavoursome recipes for wholesome soups.

Lighter soups did not become fashionable in the Netherlands until the 18th century. Inspired by the elegant sophistication and dining rituals of the much-admired French court, the French word *bouillon* was adopted to describe them. In fact, French cuisine has always had an influence on the Netherlands – the first Dutch cookbook, dating from around 1510, included translations of French recipes, and until relatively recently it was common for restaurants to present their menus in French.

The southern province of Limburg was the first to use these new light soups in the kitchens of castles, cloisters and abbeys. These soups took some time to win over the more northerly provinces of North and South Holland, however, where they were dismissed with the expression, "*water is voor de kikkers*", or "water is for frogs". Yet the 1910 Cookbook of the Amsterdam Domestic School provides recipes for no fewer than 46 soups, most of them bouillon. Soup – both light and heavy – remains a popular choice in all Dutch kitchens.

Serves 4

40g/1½oz/3 tbsp butter
1 onion, chopped
50g/2oz/½ cup plain (all-purpose) flour
1.2 litres/2 pints/5 cups milk
150g/5oz/1¼ cups grated
    mature (sharp) Gouda cheese
1 small celeriac
salt
chopped fresh chives, to garnish
toast, to serve

Alkmaar cheese soup
Alkmaarse kaassoep

Cheese tarts were made in the Netherlands as early as 1514, but cheese soups came much later, about the time of the Great Depression in the 1930s. During this period, four top Dutch chefs published a book of inexpensive recipes featuring dairy products to cater for their hungry compatriots. This soup was created by F. A. Lamers, a chef from The Hague, and it is named after the Alkmaar, the oldest cheese market in the country, in North Holland.

1 Melt the butter in a pan. Add the onion and cook over a low heat, stirring occasionally, for 5 minutes, until softened.

2 Stir in the flour and cook, stirring constantly, for 2 minutes, then gradually stir in the milk.

3 Continue to cook, stirring, until slightly thickened. Add 50g/2oz/½ cup of the grated Gouda and cook, stirring occasionally, for about 15 minutes.

4 Meanwhile, peel and finely dice the celeriac, then cook in a pan of boiling water, for about 10 minutes, until softened.

5 Drain the celeriac and add to the soup with the remaining cheese.

6 Season to taste with salt, ladle into warm soup bowls and garnish with chives. Serve immediately with toast.

Variation
This version, created by a cheese-maker from the Alblasserwaard, in South Holland, uses a farmhouse Gouda:
    Colour the Alkmaar Cheese Soup at step 2 with a little powdered saffron, and add some puréed potatoes to thicken it, and then flavour it with ½ tsp of crushed caraway seeds. Top the soup with a cheese crust made from a mixture of three crushed rusks, 200g/7oz/1¾ cups grated Gouda and a pinch of mild paprika sprinkled over. The pan should then be placed under a preheated grill (broiler) until the crust is a golden brown.

Per portion Energy 407kcal/1703kJ; Protein 21.5g; Carbohydrate 25.7g, of which sugars 15.9g; Fat 25.2g, of which saturates 16.1g; Cholesterol 71mg; Calcium 704mg; Fibre 1.4g; Sodium 582mg.

Asparagus soup
Aspergesoep

This is one of the rare Dutch soups made without meat. It is best prepared the day after serving Dutch Asparagus (see page 80), because you can then use the leftover asparagus stock, always precious because growing asparagus is tricky and labour-intensive. The Dutch saying, "He has made his asparagus beds here", means that he is here to stay.

1 Cut the asparagus spears into 5cm/2in pieces and set the tips aside in some water.

2 Bring the stock or water to the boil in a pan, add the pieces of asparagus stalk and simmer for 20 minutes. Remove the asparagus with a slotted spoon and pass through a sieve (strainer) into a bowl or process in a blender. Reserve the stock.

3 Melt the butter in a large pan over a low heat, but do not let it brown. Stir in flour and cook, stirring constantly, for 2 minutes. Gradually stir in the stock, then add the asparagus purée and the cream.

4 Strain the soup into a clean pan, then return to the heat and bring to the boil, stirring constantly.

5 Drain the asparagus tips, add them to the soup and simmer, stirring occasionally, for 10 minutes, until they are tender. Season the soup with salt and pepper and serve immediately, garnished with chopped parsley.

Variations
• The soup can also be made with chicken or veal stock.
• Instead of adding the cream to the soup, whip it and swirl it on top before serving.

Serves 4

500g/1¼lb white asparagus, peeled
  and trimmed
1.2 litres/2 pints/5 cups
  asparagus stock or water
65g/2½oz/5 tbsp butter
75g/3oz/⅔ cup plain (all-purpose) flour
120ml/4fl oz/½ cup whipping cream
salt and ground white pepper
finely chopped fresh parsley, to garnish

Per portion Energy 331kcal/1368kJ; Protein 6.1g; Carbohydrate 18g, of which sugars 3.6g; Fat 26.5g, of which saturates 16.2g; Cholesterol 66mg; Calcium 80mg; Fibre 2.7g; Sodium 108mg.

Broad bean soup
Tuinbonensoep

Serves 4

2 onions
800g/1¾lb gammon (smoked or cured
   ham), rind removed
1.2–1.6kg/2½–3½lb shelled broad
   (fava) beans
15g/½oz/1 tbsp butter
1 bunch of spring onions (scallions),
   diced
30ml/2 tbsp cornflour (cornstarch)
1 bunch of parsley, chopped
salt
single (light) cream, to serve

For the summer savory cake
(*Bonenkruidkoek*)

500g/1¼lb potatoes, peeled
2 eggs, lightly beaten
pinch of freshly grated nutmeg
30ml/2 tbsp finely chopped fresh
   summer savory
25g/1oz/2 tbsp butter
salt and ground black pepper

Variation
Take a red (bell) pepper. Remove the pits
and the stem. Divide into 4 parts, put the
skin upwards under a glowing grill until it
blackens. Peel the pepper, dice it finely
and warm in the soup for a minute before
sprinkling the soup with parsley.

Soup per portion Energy 428kcal/1793kJ; Protein
46g; Carbohydrate 26.2g, of which sugars 5.1g;
Fat 16g, of which saturates 5.2g; Cholesterol 46mg;
Calcium 108mg; Fibre 9.2g; Sodium 1777mg.

Savory cake per portion Energy 173kcal/ 727kJ;
Protein 5.5g; Carbohydrate 20.4g, of which sugars
1.8g; Fat 8.4g, of which saturates 4.2g; Cholesterol
108mg; Calcium 38mg; Fibre 1.6g; Sodium 89mg.

Long before Columbus discovered the green beans that the Dutch love, the broad bean was thriving in the vegetable gardens of Europe. These beans are not favourites with everybody – traditional nicknames include woollen mittens, farmers' toes, thick thumbs, poop beans and horse beans. However, don't let this put you off – most simply, broad beans can be enjoyed eaten with bacon, parsley and savory or in a white sauce. A more adventurous approach is this regional soup from De Achterhoek, which is best served with the summer savory cake shown here.

1 Chop one of the onions and place in a pan with the whole piece of meat and a pinch of salt. Pour in 1.5 litres/2½ pints/6¼ cups water and bring to the boil, then lower the heat and simmer for 1 hour.

2 To make the summer savory cake, rinse the potatoes and dry on kitchen paper. Coarsely grate them into a bowl, stir in the eggs, nutmeg, and savory and season.

3 Melt half the butter in a 20cm/8in diameter non-stick frying pan. Scoop the potato mixture into the pan, pressing it out evenly with a fish slice or metal spatula, and cook over a low heat until the top is dry. Loosen the edges with a knife, if necessary, and turn the cake out on to a plate.

4 Melt the remaining butter in the pan, slide the cake back into it, the cooked side uppermost, and cook until browned on the underside. Keep warm over a very low heat.

5 Remove the meat from the pan and reserve the stock. Add the beans to the pan and cook for 15–20 minutes, until tender. Meanwhile, slice the remaining onion.

6 Melt the butter in a small frying pan. Add the meat and sliced onion and cook over a low heat, stirring occasionally, for about 10 minutes, until lightly browned. Keep warm.

7 Remove half the beans from the soup and process in a food processor or blender. Stir the bean purée into the soup with the spring onions and cook for 2 minutes. Mix the cornflour to a paste with 60ml/4 tbsp water in a bowl and stir into the soup, cooking for a short time to thicken.

8 Season to taste with salt, sprinkle with the parsley and serve the soup with the summer savory cake, the meat (sliced at the table) with onion mixture and a jug (pitcher) of cream.

Groningen prawn soup
Groningse garnalensoep

Serves 2

1 small haddock, filleted with
    head and bones reserved
50g/2oz/½ cup cooked peeled
    brown prawns (shrimp)
½ rusk, crumbled
1 egg, lightly beaten
40g/1½oz/3 tbsp butter
a small piece of leek, cut into rings
15ml/1 tbsp cornflour (cornstarch)
5ml/1 tsp Groningen or Dijon mustard
15ml/1 tbsp chopped celery leaves
salt and ground black pepper
50–100g/2–3½oz/½–scant 1 cup
    cooked peeled prawns, to garnish

For the stock

½ leek
2 carrots
2 potatoes
8 celery leaves
1 bay leaf
salt

Per portion Energy 496kcal/2082kJ; Protein 43.8g;
Carbohydrate 29.7g, of which sugars 9.2g; Fat
23.8g, of which saturates 11.5g; Cholesterol 289mg;
Calcium 230mg; Fibre 1.1g; Sodium 373mg.

Delicious small brown prawns are a speciality of the north coast of Groningen as well as Zeeland. At dawn, the prawn boats steam into the harbour of Lauwersoog, where their catch is boiled in seawater aboard the vessels. This recipe, based on a dish created by Luktje Landman, a fisherman's wife from Termuntenerzijl, is the perfect way to enjoy them.

1 Cut out the gills from the fish head.

2 To make the stock, pour 750ml/1¼ pints/ 3 cups water into a pan and add the fish head and bones, leek, carrots, potatoes, celery leaves, bay leaf and a pinch of salt. Bring to the boil, then lower the heat and simmer for 30 minutes.

3 Skin and coarsely chop the haddock fillets, then process in a food processor. Scrape the fish into a bowl, add the prawns and rusk and season with salt pepper. Knead together, adding enough egg to make a firm mixture. Form into balls and leave to rest.

4 Melt the butter in a non-stick frying pan. Add the fish balls and leek rings and cook over a medium-low heat, stirring occasionally, for about 10 minutes, until they are evenly browned. Remove with a slotted spoon and set aside.

5 Add the remaining beaten egg to the pan, season with salt and cook until set like an omelette. Remove and cut into strips.

6 Using a slotted spoon, remove the fish head and bones, leek, carrots, potatoes, celery leaves and the bay leaf from the stock.

7 Dice the carrots and potatoes and return them to the soup. Then discard the remaining flavourings.

8 Mix the cornflour with 30ml/2 tbsp water to a paste in a small bowl and use it to thicken the soup. Add the mustard, celery leaves, fish balls, leek rings and egg strips. Garnish with the peeled prawns and serve.

Variation
For a simpler recipe with more fish, use 500g/1¼lb small flounders and dabs to make the stock. Place them upright with water to cover, in a covered pan with sliced leek, a bayleaf and salt. Simmer them for about 20 minutes until they are so tender that they fillet themselves when shaken by the tails. To this soup you can then add fish balls made in the same way as above, but replace the 50g/2oz/½ cup cooked peeled prawns with 250g/9oz fried prawns.

1 bottle (750ml/1¼ pints/3 cups)
   dry white wine
1 chicken leg
1 large carrot, thinly sliced
pinch of powdered saffron
4kg/8¾lb live mussels
4 onions, sliced into rings
2 bay leaves
2 celery sticks
6 black peppercorns, lightly crushed
2 leeks, thinly sliced
75g/3oz cornflour (cornstarch)
200ml/7fl oz/scant 1 cup whipping cream
salt and ground black pepper
celery leaves, to garnish
buttered soft rolls (*kadetjes*) filled with
   watercress, to serve

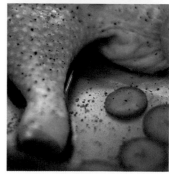

Zeeland mussel soup
Zeeuwse mosselsoep

The Dutch love affair with mussels goes back many centuries. In the 17th century, ordinary Dutch people liked to eat their mussels raw with beer for breakfast, but they were also served on the heavily loaded tables of the rich, so temptingly depicted by the famous Dutch painters of that period, such as Cornelis de Heem and Floris van Schooten.

1 Pour the wine into a large pan, add 1 litre/ 1¾ pints/4 cups water, the chicken leg, carrot and saffron and season. Bring to the boil, lower the heat, cover and simmer for 1 hour.

2 Scrub the mussels under cold water and pull off the "beards". Discard any with broken shells or those that do not shut immediately when tapped. Put them, with the onions, bay leaves, celery, peppercorns and 150ml/ ¼ pint/⅔ cup water into a pan, cover and cook over a high heat, shaking the pan three times, for 5 minutes, until the shells have opened.

3 Strain the mussels, reserving the cooking liquid. Discard any mussels that remain closed and remove the rest from their shells.

4 Strain 500ml/17fl oz/generous 2 cups of the cooking liquid through a sieve (strainer) lined with muslin (cheesecloth) twice. Add the cooking liquid to the soup.

5 Using a slotted spoon, remove the chicken leg from the pan, cut off the meat and chop finely. Add the leeks to the pan and cook for 2 minutes. Mix the cornflour with 150ml/ ¼ pint/⅔ cup water to a paste in a small bowl and stir into the soup, cooking for a short time to thicken.

6 Remove the pan from the heat and stir in the cream, mussels and chicken meat. Sprinkle with celery leaves and serve with buttered soft rolls filled with watercress.

Per portion Energy 692kcal/2910kJ; Protein 62g; Carbohydrate 32.9g, of which sugars 12.1g; Fat 22.6g, of which saturates 14.5g; Cholesterol 150mg; Calcium 712mg; Fibre 4.2g; Sodium 713mg.

Westland tomato soup
Westlandse tomatensoep

In his *Cruydt-Boeck* of 1554, Rembert Dodoens described the tomato as a "love apple" which he claimed was grown "because of its beauty" and was regarded as an aphrodisiac. The tomato was difficult to cultivate in the Dutch climate and remained too expensive for the masses until the technique of growing them under glass was developed in the Westland. Ever since that time, this soup has been a Saturday tradition in the region.

1 Put the tomatoes in a heavy pan and cook over a medium-low heat, stirring occasionally, for 10 minutes, until pulpy.

2 Pass the tomatoes through a food mill into a clean pan and heat gently, stirring occasionally, until reduced to 1 litre/ 1¾ pints/4 cups. Remove the tomatoes from the heat and set aside.

3 Melt the butter in a large pan. Add the onion and leek and cook over a low heat, stirring occasionally, for 5 minutes, until the vegetables have softened.

4 Stir in the flour to the onion and leek mixture and cook, stirring constantly, until just coloured. Gradually stir in the stock.

5 Pour in the milk and add the tomato purée and the bay leaf. Bring to the boil, stirring constantly, and lower to a simmer.

6 Season the minced steak and form into small balls. Simmer for 10 minutes in the pan.

7 Stir in the sugar and cream with the steak balls, season to taste with salt and pepper, sprinkle with chopped herbs and serve.

Serves 4

2kg/4½lb ripe tomatoes, halved
25g/1oz/2 tbsp butter
1 onion, finely chopped
1 leek, finely chopped
25g/1oz/¼ cup plain (all-purpose) flour
500ml/17fl oz/generous 2 cups hot
    beef stock
1 bay leaf
150ml/¼ pint/⅔ cup milk
200g/7oz minced (ground) steak
15ml/1 tbsp soft brown sugar
50ml/2fl oz/¼ cup whipping cream
salt and ground black pepper
chopped fresh basil, chives, parsley and
    celery leaves, to garnish

Per portion Energy 306kcal/1290kJ; Protein 17.2g; Carbohydrate 29g, of which sugars 23.5g; Fat 14.4g, of which saturates 8.9g; Cholesterol 47mg; Calcium 118mg; Fibre 6.4g; Sodium 130mg.

Serves 4

1kg/2¼lb boned and rolled meat
250g/9oz lean minced (ground) beef
1 rusk, crushed
2.5ml/½ tsp ground mace
2 onions
1 bouquet garni, consisting of 1 parsley
 sprig, 1 sage sprig and 1 bay leaf
500g/1¼lb white asparagus, peeled
100g/3¾oz vermicelli
1 bunch of celery leaves
salt

To serve

lamb's lettuce (corn salad)
cocktail onions
gherkins
lemon segments
mustard
Dutch brandy
buttered wholemeal (whole-wheat) bread

Funfair soup
Kermissoep

This substantial soup used to always be served on special occasions, such as the annual funfairs that were so popular in the southern provinces of the Netherlands. Traditionally a huge shin of beef would be served alongside rolled meat and meatballs. Fat yellow vermicelli and coarsely chopped celery leaves were also included. Sorrel, spinach, salad, parsley root and even asparagus are all ideas for flavouring the soup.

1 Put the rolled meat in a large pan, pour in 2.5 litres/4½ pints/11¼ cups water and bring to the boil. Mix together the minced beef, crushed rusk, mace and 5ml/1 tsp salt and form the mixture into small balls.

2 When the water in the pan comes to the boil, add the meatballs, onions (washed but unpeeled) and bouquet garni and skim off any scum that rises to the surface. Lower the heat and simmer for 2 hours.

3 Remove the rolled meat from the pan and leave to cool. Strain the stock through a strainer (sieve) lined with dampened muslin (cheesecloth) into a clean pan. Rinse the meatballs and return them to the stock.

4 Cut the asparagus into 5cm/2in pieces. Add to the stock and cook for 10 minutes, then add the vermicelli and cook for a further 10 minutes. Finally, add the celery leaves and season to taste with salt.

5 Make a bed of lamb's lettuce on a plate. Cut the cold rolled meat into neat slices and arrange them in the middle of the plate. Put the cocktail onions and gherkins around the rim and garnish with lemon segments.

6 Serve with buttered slices of bread with the rolled meat, mustard and pickles. Traditionally a drop of lemon juice was squeezed into the soup and spoonfuls of soup were often followed by a sip of brandy.

Per portion Energy 331kcal/1368kJ; Protein 6.1g; Carbohydrate 18g, of which sugars 3.6g; Fat 26.5g, of which saturates 16.2g, Cholesterol 66mg; Calcium 80mg; Fibre 2.7g; Sodium 108mg.

Turnip soup
Reubesoep

Even in a small country such as the Netherlands, tastes differ significantly from region to region. In the northern provinces turnips are only occasionally seen in the woods and are regarded as food for deer and wild boar, or as fodder for livestock. But in the southern provinces of Brabant and Limburg, turnips are eaten frequently, especially in spring when their taste is milder. This soup originates in Limburg where it is made with the tender Geuldal lamb that live on the moors of the region.

1 Put the lamb, rosemary and bay leaves in a large pan, add 1.5 litres/2½ pints/6¼ cups water, season and bring to the boil. Lower the heat, cover and simmer for 3 hours.

2 Discard the rosemary and bay leaves from the stock. Add the turnips, carrots and potatoes to the pan, re-cover and simmer for a further 15 minutes, until the vegetables are tender but retain some "bite".

3 Dry-fry the smoked streaky bacon in a heavy frying pan until crisp. Remove the bacon from the pan, drain on kitchen paper.

4 Ladle the soup into soup bowls, garnish with the chervil and bacon and serve.

Cook's tip
Serve with *soldaatjes* (little soldiers), strips of stale bread browned in butter.

Serves 4

300g/11oz boneless shin
   (shank) of lamb, diced
1 rosemary sprig
4 bay leaves
500g/1¼lb young turnips, diced
100g/3¾oz carrots, diced
100g/3¾oz potatoes, diced
salt and ground black pepper

To garnish

8 thin slices smoked
   streaky (fatty) bacon
chopped fresh chervil

Per portion Energy 345kcal/1437kJ; Protein 25.3g; Carbohydrate 11.9g, of which sugars 7.8g; Fat 22.2g, of which saturates 8.6g; Cholesterol 94mg; Calcium 77mg; Fibre 3.9g; Sodium 801mg.

Queen's soup
Koninginnesoep

Serves 4

1 boiling fowl (stewing chicken)
7.5ml/1½ tsp salt
1 small leek
1 tarragon sprig, plus extra to garnish
1 chervil sprig
1 thyme sprig
1 mace blade
65g/2½oz/⅓ cup rice
50ml/2fl oz/¼ cup egg yolk
50ml/2fl oz/¼ cup whipping cream

Variations

• Using tarragon as a garnish is a homage to Queen Wilhelmina of the Netherlands (1890–1948) who was especially fond of this herb.
• The soup is also made with a base of roux, using 40g butter and 50g flour. This is seasoned with an egg yolk and cream, and a dash of white Bordeaux wine.

Per portion Energy 369kcal/1547kJ; Protein 48.8g; Carbohydrate 14g, of which sugars 0.9g; Fat 13g, of which saturates 5.4g; Cholesterol 328mg; Calcium 45mg; Fibre 0.6g; Sodium 160mg.

This is a variation of a French recipe, originally named after the wife of Henry IV, La Reine Marguérite. It was very popular in the Netherlands during the 1940s. Up until that time, all restaurant menus were written in French because this was considered more refined. This changed, however, when the occupying Germans banned the French language from restaurants and cookbooks during World War II. The Dutch responded by ordering this soup in restaurants during the war as a mark of patriotism to the Dutch Queen Wilhelmina, who was exiled in Britain.

1 Put the boiling fowl, salt, leek, tarragon, chervil, thyme and mace in a large pan and add 1.5 litres/2½ pint/6¼ cups water. Bring to the boil, then lower the heat, cover and simmer for 2 hours.

2 Remove the boiling fowl from the pan and leave to cool. Pass the stock through a strainer (sieve) lined with dampened muslin (cheesecloth) into a clean pan. Add the rice, bring to the boil and cook for 30 minutes, until it is tender.

3 Ladle the soup into a food processor, in batches if necessary, and process. Alternatively, pass it through a food mill. Return the soup to the pan.

4 Remove the meat from the bones and dice neatly. Add the chicken to the pan and bring the soup to the boil again.

5 Remove the pan from the heat. Beat the egg yolk with a ladleful of the soup, then stir it into the pan with the cream. Warm through gently, but do not let it boil. Sprinkle with tarragon and serve immediately.

Variation
This soup can be made using a roux, with 40g/1½oz/3 tbsp butter and 50g/2oz/½ cup plain (all-purpose) flour. The roux should then be thickened with an egg yolk and cream and finally flavoured with a dash of white Bordeaux wine.

Pea soup
Erwtensoep

When the canals and lakes freeze over in the winter months, everybody goes skating and little stalls appear, offering skaters the chance to warm up with a cup of pea soup. There are many variations of this dish. Most Dutch follow the province of Guelderland in using smoked sausage, but the Frisians in the north prefer fresh sausages.

1 Rinse the peas under cold running water and place in a large pan. Add 2.5 litres/4¼ pints/10⅔ cups water, bring to the boil and skim off any scum that rises to the surface.

2 Add the gammon, spare ribs, pig's trotter and bacon, season with salt and simmer over a low heat for about 3 hours, until the meat is tender. Remove the bacon from the pan and leave to cool.

3 Peel and dice the celeriac. Chop half the celery leaves and reserve the remainder for garnish. Add the celeriac, chopped celery leaves, leeks and carrot to the soup and simmer for 30 minutes, until tender.

4 Put the smoked sausage in a pan, add enough water to cover and poach the sausage over a very low heat for approximately 20 minutes.

5 Using a slotted spoon, remove the meat from the soup. Cut the meat from the bones and dice it. Return the meat to the soup and add the sausage.

6 Serve the soup in bowls and garnish each one with the reserved celery leaves.

7 As a tasty accompaniment, slice the bacon and serve on thin slices of rye bread spread with mustard.

800g/1¾lb/3½ cups green split peas
500g/1¼lb uncured gammon
  (fresh ham)
250g/9oz pork spare ribs
1 split pig's trotter (foot)
250g/9oz lean bacon in a single piece
1 small celeriac
1 bunch of celery leaves
500g/1¼lb leeks, thickly sliced
1 carrot, sliced
1 smoked (Guelders) sausage,
  about 250g/9oz
salt
rye bread spread with mustard, to serve

Per portion Energy 914kcal/3843kJ; Protein 68.5g; Carbohydrate 87g, of which sugars 8.4g; Fat 34.8g, of which saturates 12.5g; Cholesterol 75mg; Calcium 222mg; Fibre 18.1g; Sodium 2216mg.

Runner bean soup
Humkessoep

The Dutch name for this dish, *humkessoep*, uses the dialect from the eastern part of the country. The soup itself is a direct legacy of the tradition of cooking meals over an open fire. The white beans were in season at harvest time, so the soup was often made as a festive dish. It should be served with buttered white bread – which used to be a luxury – and topped with a thin slice of *naegelholt*, a dried piece of silverside spiced with nutmeg or cloves.

1 After soaking, drain the white beans and rinse under cold running water.

2 Put the rib of beef in a large pan, add 2 litres/3½ pints/8¾ cups water and a pinch of salt and bring the pan to the boil. After having skimmed off any scum that rises to the surface, lower the heat and simmer for 1 hour.

3 Add the white beans to the pan, re-cover and simmer for 1 hour more.

4 Peel and thickly dice the celeriac.

5 Add the runner beans, potatoes, leeks and celeriac to the soup and simmer for 20 minutes, until tender. Taste, adjust the seasoning, and garnish with chopped herbs.

6 Carve the meat into slices and serve with the buttered bread and soup.

Variation
The stock can also be made from pork. You will need 500g/1¼lb pork spare ribs, 300g/11oz fresh sausage and 100g/3¾oz lean smoked bacon. You can also use other kinds of green beans.

Serves 4

250g/9oz/1⅓ cups dried white beans, soaked in cold water for 12 hours
800g/1¾lb rib of beef
800g/1¾lb celeriac
800g/1¾lb runner (green) beans, cut into short lengths
250g/9oz potatoes, thickly diced
2 leeks, thickly diced
salt
chopped fresh parsley or celery leaves, to garnish
buttered white bread, to serve

Per portion Energy 462kcal/1952kJ; Protein 43.2g; Carbohydrate 48.4g, of which sugars 11.7g; Fat 12g, of which saturates 4.3g; Cholesterol 58mg; Calcium 240mg; Fibre 18.6g; Sodium 204mg.

Sunday soup
Zondagse groentensoep

Serves 4

1 onion
2 cloves
400g/14oz shin (shank) of beef with bone
1 bunch of parsley
bay leaf
150g/5oz minced (ground) veal
15ml/1 tbsp breadcrumbs or rusk crumbs
pinch of freshly grated nutmeg
400g/14oz mixed diced vegetables, such
  as carrots, leeks, green beans and
  cauliflower or winter vegetables such
  as celeriac and Brussels sprouts
40g/1½oz broken vermicelli
salt and ground black pepper
chopped fresh parsley, to garnish

Per portion Energy 318kcal/1330kJ; Protein 32.4g;
Carbohydrate 19.8g, of which sugars 8.4g; Fat
12.4g, of which saturates 5g; Cholesterol 81mg;
Calcium 44mg; Fibre 2.7g; Sodium 150mg.

The Dutch have always had a strong Christian culture, and church on Sundays was an essential part of the weekly routine. Whatever your denomination, this substantial soup was always served for dinner afterwards, a luxury that you could not expect on a weekday. This soup has always been a children's favourite. When coming home from school on Saturday, children would know that the weekend had started because a pot of broth was simmering on the cooker.

1 Stud the unpeeled onion with the cloves. Put the beef in a pan, add 1.5 litres/2½ pints/ 6¼ cups water and bring to the boil.

2 Skim off any scum that rises to the surface of the pan and add the onion, parsley and bay leaf and season with salt and pepper. Lower the heat, cover and simmer for 3 hours.

3 Remove the beef from the pan, cut the meat off the bone and dice it.

4 Strain the stock through a sieve (strainer) lined with dampened muslin (cheesecloth) into a clean pan.

5 Mix together the veal, breadcrumbs and nutmeg in a bowl and season with salt. Form the mixture into small meatballs.

6 Bring the stock to the boil again, add the meatballs, diced vegetables and vermicelli and cook for 15 minutes, until the vegetables are tender.

7 Add the beef to the pan and warm the mixture through.

8 Season to taste with salt and pepper, garnish with chopped parsley and serve immediately.

Variations
• You can use 40g/1½oz/scant ¼ cup pre-boiled rice instead of vermicelli, adding it with the vegetables in step 6.
• You can thicken the soup with 15ml/2 tbsp potato flour or cornflour (cornstarch).

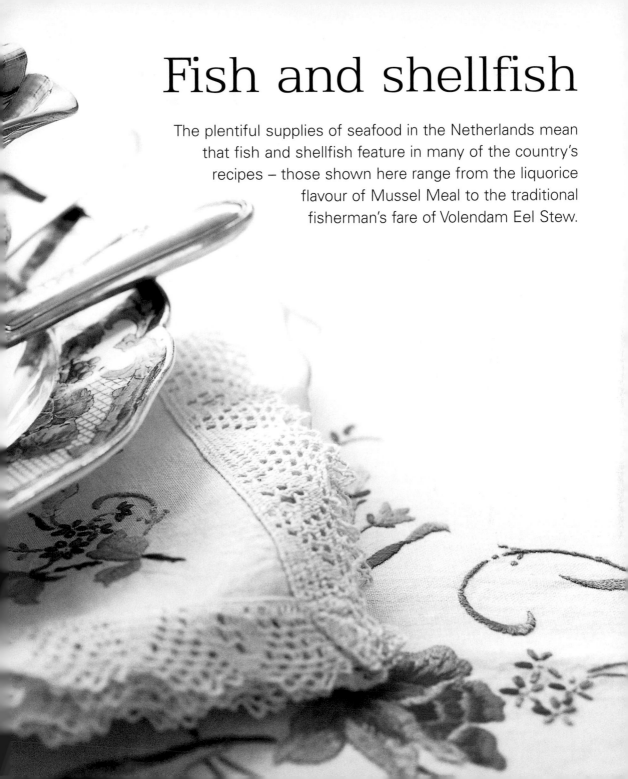

Fish and shellfish

The plentiful supplies of seafood in the Netherlands mean that fish and shellfish feature in many of the country's recipes – those shown here range from the liquorice flavour of Mussel Meal to the traditional fisherman's fare of Volendam Eel Stew.

Zander, stockfish
and mussels

In the medieval period, fish dishes were not popularly eaten by the Dutch. Advice at the time said that you should avoid fish broth (even made with wine) in sauces and stews, because it would always taste of fish. This seems strange in a country with a rich history of fishing and seafaring. Part of the reason for this was because, before refrigerators, fish had a very limited shelf life and so was seen as less appetizing – a traditional Dutch expression says that "Guests and fish stay fresh for only three days".

This view of fish lasted for centuries and changed only relatively recently – even during the 1920s, when meat was scarce, the government worked hard to persuade the Dutch to eat more fish. The explanation was simply that fish was seen as second-best – it was always eaten because the population could not afford meat. Also, fish tended to be eaten on Fridays and during Lent when meat was banned by the Roman Catholic Church. So the smell of fish was associated with church rituals as well as poverty. There is a Dutch expression "butter with the fish", meaning that fish tastes much better when served in a wealthy household who can afford butter with which to serve it.

Thanks to the low calorie and healthy omega-3 content of fish, this ingredient has now become widely popular and fashionable. Most Dutch households now serve fish once a week. Freshness is no longer an issue because in almost every village, there is a twice-weekly fish stall with a selection of herring, eel, salmon, whiting, cod, haddock, brown prawns, smoked mackerel, eel and buckling, all well chilled. Every major city also has fish restaurants, where you can dine out on your favourite.

The effectiveness of modern fishing techniques means that certain species of fish, such as eels and cod, have now become endangered, although various measures are being introduced to keep these fish on our tables.

1 plaice or flounder,
  1kg/2¼lb
1 carrot, chopped
1 leek, chopped
1 branch celery, chopped
1 bay leaf
5ml/1 tsp parsley
50g/2oz/¼ cup butter,
  plus extra for greasing
juice of 1 lemon
freshly grated nutmeg
4 thin lemon slices
4 coarsely cut sage leaves
4 rusks, crushed
chives, to garnish
salt and ground black pepper

To serve

dressed green salad
crusty bread
sugar, for sprinkling

Frisian plaice
Friese schol

The housekeeper of a wealthy Frisian family first recorded this recipe in 1772. The Frisians, from the West Frisian islands on the north edge of the country, are regarded by the Dutch as rather uncompromising characters with idiosyncratic ways, and their own language. This is a popular recipe – as many as ten top Amsterdam chefs recommended a similar recipe to this in *Het Kook-en Huishoudboek*, a famous cookbook published in 1908.

1 Cut off the tail and head from the fish with a sharp knife and snip off the fins with kitchen scissors. Remove and discard the gills. Put the fish trimmings and the chopped carrot, leek and celery with the bay leaf and parsley in a large pan, season and add water to cover. Bring to the boil, then lower the heat, cover and simmer for 1 hour. Strain the stock into a bowl and leave to cool.

2 Preheat the oven to 200°C/400°F/Gas 6. Grease an ovenproof dish with butter. Cut the fish into six thick strips and push out the guts. Add the lemon juice to a bowl of water, rinse the fish strips, and pat dry with kitchen paper.

3 Sprinkle the fish strips with nutmeg and season with salt and pepper.

4 Place the strips upright, with the cut sides underneath them, in the prepared dish and tuck the lemon slices in between.

5 Measure 200ml/7fl oz/scant 1 cup of the fish stock and pour it around the fish.

6 Sprinkle with the sage and cover the crushed rusks. Dot the butter over the top and bake for 20 minutes. Garnish the fish with chopped chives, and sprinkle the salad with sugar, before serving.

Per portion Energy 325kcal/1358kJ; Protein 27.6g; Carbohydrate 21.2g, of which sugars 8.4g; Fat 14.9g, of which saturates 7g; Cholesterol 94mg; Calcium 208mg; Fibre 0.6g; Sodium 259mg.

North Holland salad
Noord-Hollandse slaschotel

This is the perfect main dish for a hot summer's day, when the sublime North Holland potato Opperdoezer Ronde is in season. This firm yellow potato is a perfect partner for this salad with the refreshing herrings presented on round lettuce. This classic lettuce matches up to any modern one – taste a piece of its heart and you will discover why.

1 Scrape the potatoes, remove the "eyes" and cook in plenty of boiling water for about 20 minutes, until tender. Drain well and keep warm.

2 Tear the lettuce into bitesize pieces and spread out on a serving platter. Arrange the egg halves and strips of cheese on top.

3 Cut the herrings into small squares and add to the platter.

4 Sprinkle the herrings with the spring onions and gherkins.

5 Whisk together the oil and vinegar in a bowl, season with salt and pepper and sprinkle the dressing over the salad. Garnish with chopped parsley.

6 Serve with the potatoes and a sauceboat of the melted butter, with mustard, oil and vinegar added to taste.

Serves 2

6–8 Opperdoezer Ronde or
    other waxy potatoes
1 round (butterhead) lettuce, coarse
    outer leaves removed
2 hard-boiled eggs, halved
100g/3¾oz extra-mature (sharp)
    Gouda cheese, cut into thin strips
4 marinated herrings, drained
2 spring onions (scallions),
    coarsely chopped
4 large sweet pickled gherkins,
    cut into strips
45ml/3 tbsp olive oil
15ml/1 tbsp white wine vinegar
salt and ground black pepper
chopped fresh parsley, to garnish

To serve

boiled potatoes
50g/2oz/¼ cup butter, melted
mustard, oil and vinegar

Per portion Energy 862kcal/3577kJ; Protein 38g;
Carbohydrate 21g, of which sugars 13.5g; Fat 69.8g,
of which saturates 27.3g; Cholesterol 328mg;
Calcium 477mg; Fibre 1.9g; Sodium 1525mg.

Zander with parsley sauce
Snoekbaars met peterseliesaus

Serves 4

4 zander or pike-perch
   fillets, each about 250g/9oz,
   head and bones reserved
1 onion
1 carrot
1 parsley sprig
6 black peppercorns
5ml/1 tsp ground mace
15ml/1 tbsp chopped fresh thyme
300g/11oz potatoes, sliced
300g/11oz celeriac, diced
200g/7oz carrots, sliced
200g/7oz mangetouts (snow peas)
200g/7oz leeks, sliced
75g/3oz/6 tbsp butter
50g/2oz/½ cup plain (all-purpose) flour
30ml/2 tbsp milk
30ml/2 tbsp finely chopped fresh parsley
salt and ground black pepper

Per portion Energy 565kcal/2362kJ; Protein 52.1g;
Carbohydrate 30.7g, of which sugars 9g; Fat 26.7g,
of which saturates 15.5g; Cholesterol 177mg;
Calcium 151mg; Fibre 5.8g; Sodium 398mg.

During World War II, the Dutch were able to buy fish without coupons as well as catch it for themselves, so freshwater fish became a delicacy in those times of hardship. This recipe for zander, also known as pike perch, is described in several wartime cookbooks. This dish is inspired by a popular interpretation of this recipe by the chef Albert Tielemans.

1 Put the fish head and bones in a pan with the onion, carrot, parsley and peppercorns. Add 400ml/14 fl oz/1⅔ cups water and bring to the boil. Cover and simmer for 20 minutes.

2 Strain the stock into a pan and bring to just below boiling point. Sprinkle the skin of the fish with the mace and thyme and season. Fold the fillets in half, skin side inwards, and tie with kitchen string. Add the fillets to the stock and poach for 10 minutes.

3 Remove the fish from the pan with a slotted spoon. Cut off and discard the string and keep the fish warm. Reserve the stock.

4 Cook the potatoes and celeriac together in boiling water for 15–20 minutes, until tender.

5 Cook the carrots, mangetouts and leeks in separate pans of boiling water, each with 15g/½oz/1 tbsp of the butter, until tender.

6 Drain the potato and celeriac mixture and mash well. Season to taste with salt and then stir in 25g/1oz/2 tbsp of the remaining butter.

7 Spoon the mash into a piping (pastry) bag and pipe a decorative ring on a serving plate. Place the fish in the middle.

8 Drain the carrots, mangetouts and leeks and arrange between the fish on the plate.

9 Melt the remaining butter in a small pan. Stir in the flour and cook over a low heat, stirring constantly, until it is just coloured. Then gradually stir in the reserved fish stock.

10 Continue cooking the sauce, stirring constantly, until it thickens. Stir in the milk and parsley, pour the sauce over the fish and serve immediately.

Red gurnard with asparagus
Poon met asperges

Serves 4

8 red gurnards, 100g/3¾oz each
150g/5oz powdered droge worst or
   other dried sausage
30ml/2 tbsp white breadcrumbs

For the asparagus

8 white asparagus spears, trimmed
salt
15g/½oz/1 tbsp butter
30ml/2 tbsp lemon juice

For the celeriac sauce

50g/2oz celeriac, diced
150ml/¼ pint/⅔ cup fish stock
50ml/2fl oz/¼ cup double (heavy) cream
50ml/2fl oz/¼ cup sour cream
salt and ground black pepper

Cook's tip

Droge worst is a dried pork sausage,
heavily flavoured with cloves. It is thinly
sliced and dried until crisp in a medium
oven, then processed to a powder.

Per portion Energy 489kcal/2043kJ; Protein 44.8g;
Carbohydrate 11.2g, of which sugars 3g; Fat 29.7g,
of which saturates 11.2g; Cholesterol 55mg; Calcium
218mg; Fibre 1.5g; Sodium 600mg.

Maintaining the standard and vibrancy of any national cuisine involves
more than reproducing successful recipes of the past. It is also important
to adapt to modern trends and research. This recipe is based on one by
Jonnie Boer, one of the most creative young contemporary chefs in the
Netherlands, who runs the renowned restaurant De Librije in Overijssel in
the east of the country. He is inspired by regional products and traditional
recipes, and aims for carefully balanced innovation in all his dishes.

1 First, prepare the garnish. Peel the
asparagus carefully with a vegetable peeler
from the tip. Poach gently in boiling, salted
water for 10 minutes.

2 Remove the pan from the heat and leave
to rest in the cooking liquid for at least 20
minutes, then drain well. Place in a dish, add
the butter and lemon juice, season with salt
and pepper and keep warm.

3 For the sauce, put the celeriac, stock and
double cream in a pan and cook over a
medium heat for 15–20 minutes, until tender.

4 Transfer the mixture to a blender and
process until smooth, then pass through a
sieve (strainer) into a clean pan. Bring to the
boil, add the sour cream and season. Remove
the pan from the heat and keep warm.

5 Preheat the oven to 160°C/325°F/Gas 3.
Cut off the gurnard tails from just behind
the last fin. Discard the heads and front
parts of the fish.

6 Heat a non-stick frying pan, add the fish,
in batches if necessary, and cook until
lightly browned on both sides. Remove
the fish from the pan.

7 Mix together the powdered sausage and
breadcrumbs. Coat the fish with the mixture
and place on a baking sheet. The coating will
cling better to the fish if you make 10
shallow incisions with a very sharp knife on
the top side.

8 Bake for 6–12 minutes, until the flesh
flakes easily with a fork. Serve immediately
with the asparagus and celeriac sauce.

300ml/½ pint/1¼ cups Rhine wine
300ml/½ pint/1¼ cups freshly
    squeezed orange juice
30ml/2 tbsp finely chopped white onion
10ml/2 tsp grated orange rind
pinch of ground cinnamon, plus
    extra to garnish
pinch of ground ginger
4 salmon fillets, each about 175g/6oz
25g/1oz/2 tbsp butter
salt
2 oranges, thinly sliced, to garnish
boiled rice, to serve

Salmon with orange
Zalm met sinaasappel

This dish could easily have been created in the last decade of the 20th century, when everyone was inspired by Mediterranean cuisine. In fact, the idea of orange juice combined with fish was introduced by a doctor called Carel Baten as early as 1593. The idea most probably came to him via Sicily, from where the then bitter oranges were imported into the Netherlands. Sicilians still prepare fish *all' arancia*, so the combination is associated with the Mediterranean as well as northern Europe.

1 Pour the wine and orange juice into a pan, add the onion, orange rind, cinnamon and ginger and season with salt. Bring to the boil, then lower the heat, cover and simmer for 10 minutes.

2 Add the salmon to the pan, cover and poach gently for 10 minutes. Using a fish slice or metal slotted spatula, transfer the fish to a heatproof dish and keep warm.

3 Bring the cooking liquid back to the boil and cook until thickened and reduced.

4 Season the sauce with salt, stir in the butter and ladle the sauce over the salmon.

5 Garnish the salmon with thin unpeeled orange slices, sprinkled with cinnamon. Serve the salmon dish immediately with boiled rice.

Per portion Energy 347kcal/1445kJ; Protein 21.5g; Carbohydrate 12.8g, of which sugars 12.6g; Fat 18.4g, of which saturates 6.5g; Cholesterol 69mg; Calcium 67mg; Fibre 1.2g; Sodium 112mg.

Volendam eel stew
Volendammer zootje

Eel fishing typically takes place in the IJsselmeer, or Lake IJssel, a shallow dike-enclosed lake in the north of the Netherlands. Volendam, an old fishing village that looks on to the IJsselmeer, with its charming fishermen's houses and narrow canals, is particularly known for its delicious eel, which can be bought freshly caught, smoked or baked. This Volendam Eel Stew was originally a fisherman's meal, as it was easy to prepare in the small galley of ships.

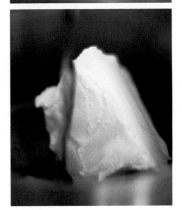

1 Put the potatoes into a large pan and pour in 400ml/14fl oz/1⅔ cups water. Put the pieces of eel on top of the potatoes, cover and cook over a very low heat for about 20 minutes, until potatoes are tender.

2 Meanwhile, make the sauce. Melt the butter with the vinegar over a very low heat and season with salt and pepper.

3 Ladle the potatoes and eels on to warm plates, preferably ones with holes, placed on top of other plates.

4 Transfer the sauce to small bowls and place one on each plate. Serve immediately.

Variation

In Marken, an island opposite Volendam, they use the following preparation:

Pack 500g/1¼lb eel, cut into small pieces upright in a small, rinsed-out pan. Season with black pepper and cook over a low heat for about 5 minutes, until the fat starts to run.

Add 125g/4¼oz/8½ tbsp butter and a small dash of vinegar. Cover and cook until the liquid has evaporated. Sprinkle the eel with two crushed rusks.

Serve with the Volendam sauce mixed with half a crumbled cooked potato. Eat this with your fingers, accompanied by rice porridge sprinkled with sugar.

Serves 4

1kg/2¼lb waxy potatoes, cut into pieces
8 eels, skinned, cleaned and cut into pieces

For the sauce

100g/3¾/2oz /scant ½ cup butter
100ml/3¾/2fl oz/scant ½ cup vinegar
salt and ground black pepper

Cook's tip

To eat, spear the potatoes with a fork and dip them in the sauce. For the eel, use clean hands to dip the eel in the sauce.

Per portion Energy 613kcal/2560kJ; Protein 29.3g; Carbohydrate 40.4g, of which sugars 3.4g; Fat 38.3g, of which saturates 17.6g; Cholesterol 278mg; Calcium 48mg; Fibre 2.5g; Sodium 313mg.

Mussel meal
Mosselmaal

Serves 2

2 fennel bulbs, trimmed and quartered
2 celery sticks, coarsely chopped
1 onion, coarsely chopped
1 bay leaf
1 thyme sprig
300ml/½ pint/1¼ cups dry white wine
2kg/4½lb live mussels
15ml/1 tbsp finely chopped fresh chervil
15ml/1 tbsp Pernod
white pepper

To serve (optional)

white bread
gherkins
mayonnaise flavoured with Pernod
chips (French fries)
winter salad (see Cook's tip)

Cook's tip

For a winter salad, mix thin strips of carrot in a dressing of two parts olive oil to one part wine vinegar, seasoned with pepper, salt and a pinch of sugar. Toss with sliced iceberg lettuce and strips of red cabbage.

Per portion Energy 179kcal/752kJ; Protein 5.7g; Carbohydrate 30.3g, of which sugars 5.2g; Fat 4.8g, of which saturates 2.5g; Cholesterol 34mg; Calcium 104mg; Fibre 0.8g; Sodium 301mg.

This delightful dish from Zeeuws Vlaanderen in southern Zeeland combines the taste for fennel liquorice shared by all Dutch children with an adult passion for wine and French pernod. The Zeeland cuisine has been considerably influenced by the Huguenot refugees who moved there in the 17th century, and who gave their local dishes a French touch.

1 Put the fennel, celery, onion, bay leaf and thyme in a large, heavy pan, pour in the wine and simmer for about 20 minutes, until tender. Bring the liquid to the boil and cook until reduced by half.

2 Meanwhile, scrub the mussels under cold running water and pull off the "beards". Discard any mussels with broken shells or any that do not shut immediately when sharply tapped.

3 Add the mussels to the pan, season with pepper, cover and cook over a high heat, shaking the pan three times, for about 10 minutes, until the shells have opened. Remove and discard any mussels that remain closed. Sprinkle with chervil and Pernod.

4 Serve immediately with white bread, gherkins and mayonnaise flavoured with Pernod. Alternatively, do it the Belgian way with a generous supply of chips. You can also serve the dish with a winter salad.

Variation

The more traditional national way to eat mussels in the Netherlands uses the following recipe:

Prepare and cook the vegetables and herbs in 150ml/¼ pint/⅔ cup water or white wine (see step 1), substituting celery leaves and a carrot for the fennel and celery sticks.

Then prepare and cook the mussels (see steps 2 to 3).

Serve the mussels from the pan with a selection of mayonnaise sauces flavoured with mustard, tomato purée (paste), chopped herbs, capers or crème fraîche.

Serve the mussels with crusty bread and a salad as a side dish. The mussels should be eaten by picking them up with an empty shell, and then dipping them into the sauce.

De Achterhoek stockfish
Achterhoekse stokvis

Serves 4

250g/9oz stockfish
500g/1¼lb waxy potatoes
40g/1½oz/3 tbsp butter
4 onions, sliced
400g/14oz/3½ cups finely shredded
  red cabbage
1 tart apple, peeled, cored and quartered
15ml/1 tbsp red wine vinegar
2 cloves
pinch of sugar
salt and ground black pepper

For the mustard sauce

25g/1oz/2 tbsp butter
25g/1oz/¼ cup plain (all-purpose) flour
400ml/14fl oz fish stock
30ml/2 tbsp Dutch or Dijon mustard

Stockfish is cod that has been dried until it is stiff and hard, similar to salt cod. In the past it used to be pounded with hammers for 24 hours before soaking, but today you can buy the fish ready to cook from good fish suppliers. In De Achterhoek, in the eastern part of the Netherlands, it was traditionally used as a festive dish for weddings and birthday parties, during fairs and at the end of the rye harvest.

1 Soak the fish in a large bowl of cold water for 24 hours, changing the water two or three times.

2 Drain the fish, pull off the skin and remove the bones.

3 Cut the fish into 15cm/6in long strips, then roll up the strips and tie with kitchen string.

4 Bring a pan of salted water to the boil, add the fish rolls and poach for 45–60 minutes, until the fish is cooked through.

5 Cook the potatoes in salted boiling water for 20–25 minutes, until tender.

6 Meanwhile, melt the butter in a large, heavy frying pan with 200ml/7fl oz water. Add the onions and cook over a low heat, stirring occasionally, for 10 minutes, until lightly browned.

7 Put the cabbage, apple, vinegar, cloves and sugar in a pan, season with salt and pepper, and cook over a medium heat for 20 minutes, until tender.

8 To make the sauce, melt the butter in a pan over a low heat. Stir in the flour and cook, stirring constantly until lightly coloured.

9 Gradually stir the stock into the sauce and simmer, stirring constantly, for a further minute until slightly thickened. Stir in the mustard.

10 Drain the potatoes. Transfer the fish and vegetables to a warm serving dish and serve immediately with the sauce in a sauceboat handed separately.

Variation
Instead of vinegar, you can add a dash of red wine with a tablespoon of currants to the cabbage at step 7.

Per portion Energy 440kcal/1846kJ; Protein 28.1g; Carbohydrate 48.8g, of which sugars 20.1g; Fat 16.7g, of which saturates 8.8g; Cholesterol 72mg; Calcium 145mg; Fibre 6.6g; Sodium 376mg.

Main dishes

In this section you will find recipes using the three essential features of the Dutch diet – potatoes, vegetables and meat – in creations ranging from Kale with Smoked Sausage, the country's signature dish, to the classic Sunday recipe for Mum's Braising Steak.

Potatoes, vegetables and meat – the Dutch triplet

In the period leading up to the 1950s a familiar household scene would have been long rows of colourful jars with home-preserved summer vegetables, meat and fruit in the cellar, together with bulging jute sacks of potatoes, and apples and stewing pears spread out on the floor of the attic. Meat also used to be dried, smoked or pickled, and eggs were kept in water glass (sodium silicate). It was impossible to get through the winter without such a collection of preserved ingredients.

Modern technology has now made these domestic rituals unnecessary. Despite this, traditional dishes are still based on the ingredients of the past, and this is why the Dutch still like smoked, pickled and dried meat, as well as vegetables and fruit, as part of their diet. It is a matter of collective nostalgia. This chapter features the three key features of Dutch cooking – potatoes, vegetables and meat.

As early as 1588, potatoes were introduced to the Netherlands from Vienna, but the plant remained a curiosity and an occasional speciality in the diet of the upper classes. In this period, the standard accompaniment to the main meal was bread. The potato did not become popular until the end of the 18th century in the face of famine caused by repeated wheat-crop failures. This established the potato as a staple food. Now the Dutch have become real potato connoisseurs and at least 44 different varieties are available to them.

The Dutch love to pile their plates with huge quantities of vegetables and are often amazed by what they consider as the minute portions of greens served by other European countries. As a seafaring nation, the Dutch were quick to discover the importance of eating fresh vegetables and fruit so sailors could avoid scurvy, and after the discovery of vitamin C in 1928, campaigns were launched to promote the consumption of fruit and vegetables. All this has made the Dutch top producers and consumers of vegetables and fruit.

The third essential element of a good main course in the Netherlands is meat. Its availability was generally dependent on the surrounding landscape – in areas unsuitable for cattle rearing, meatless days were not uncommon, whereas regions with plenty of flat meadowland for raising cattle had plentiful supplies.

Dutch asparagus
Asperges op z'n Hollands

In the early 20th century, a priest began cultivating the first white asparagus in Limburg to raise money for his parishioners. Now, both Limburg and Brabant have an Asparagus Society, and these organize peeling competitions as well as asparagus feasts. From the middle of May the N271 in Limburg, christened the "asparagus road", is dotted with stalls selling the vegetable. At the end of the season, on 24 June, there is even a mass celebrated in St Jan's Cathedral in 's-Hertogenbosch to bid the vegetable farewell.

1 Rinse the asparagus and trim about 2cm/¾in from the base, reserving the trimmings. Using a vegetable peeler, carefully peel the spears from the tips downwards. Put the peel and trimmings in a pan and cover with a clean dish towel, leaving the sides overhanging.

2 Place the asparagus spears on the dish towel, fold in the overhang and add cold water to cover and the salt. Cover the pan and bring to the boil, then lower the heat and poach gently for 10 minutes.

3 Remove the pan from the heat and leave to stand for 15–20 minutes. Test the asparagus is tender by pricking the ends with a fork; they should be soft but not mushy.

4 Meanwhile, cook the potatoes in a pan of boiling water for 20 minutes, until tender. Drain and keep warm.

5 Hard-boil the eggs in another pan of boiling water for 10 minutes. Refresh under cold running water, shell and halve.

6 Using a slotted spoon, remove the asparagus from the pan and drain on a dish towel. Pour the melted butter into a sauceboat.

7 Arrange the asparagus spears on individual plates and garnish with ham, hard-boiled egg halves and warm potatoes sprinkled with nutmeg and chopped parsley. Serve immediately with the melted butter.

Serves 4

2kg/4½lb finest white asparagus
25ml/1½ tbsp salt
8–12 small new potatoes, peeled
4 eggs
8 slices unsmoked cooked ham
100g/3¾oz/scant ½ cup butter, melted
pinch of freshly grated nutmeg
chopped fresh parsley, to garnish

Cook's tip
After purchasing asparagus, place it in cold water, changing the water frequently. After a few hours, the stems will have absorbed so much liquid that they will become juicy and easy to peel.

Per portion Energy 491kcal/2035kJ; Protein 31.4g; Carbohydrate 22.7g, of which sugars 11.1g; Fat 31g, of which saturates 15.7g; Cholesterol 273mg; Calcium 176mg; Fibre 9.3g; Sodium 835mg.

Serves 4

40g/1½oz/3 tbsp butter, softened,
   plus extra for greasing
100g/3¾oz/scant 1 cup plain
   (all-purpose) flour, plus extra for
   dusting
100g/3¾oz/scant 1 cup self-raising
   (self-rising) flour
2.5ml/½ tsp salt
100ml/3½fl oz/scant ½ cup white wine
beaten egg, for brushing

For the filling

300g/11oz/1⅓ cups fresh cream cheese
2.5ml/½ tsp salt
4 large (US extra large) eggs
90g/3½oz/scant 2 cups chopped
   fresh chervil
15ml/1 tbsp chopped fresh chives
15ml/1 tbsp chopped fresh tarragon

Per portion Energy 672kcal/2793kJ; Protein 14.1g;
Carbohydrate 39.4g, of which sugars 1.6g; Fat
50.4g, of which saturates 29.1g; Cholesterol 283mg;
Calcium 289mg; Fibre 3.1g; Sodium 703mg.

Chervil pie
Kerveltaart

Chervil pie is not a novelty dish, but a long-established recipe. A savoury
pie such as this tends to be associated with the French, and is sometimes
known as quiche, but this recipe is an updated version of one from a
Dutch cookbook written in the 16th century.

1 Preheat the oven to 200°C/400°F/Gas 6.
Grease a 28cm/11in loose-based fluted
flan tin (pan) with butter.

2 Sift both types of flour and the salt into a
bowl. Stir in the butter and wine with a knife
and knead quickly to form a smooth and
elastic dough. (You may need to add a little
more wine or flour.) Roll out the dough on a
lightly floured surface to a 33cm/13in round.

3 Line the tin with the dough and trim the
edge, so that the pastry case (pie shell) is no
deeper than 3cm/1¼in. Brush with beaten
egg. Place the flan tin on a baking sheet.

4 Beat the cream cheese until smooth, then
beat in the salt and eggs, one at a time. Stir
in the herbs and spoon the filling into the
pastry case. Bake for about 45 minutes,
until golden and the filling has set.

Variation

Use the same dough to make many other
vegetarian pies and, at the same time, take
the opportunity to sample different Dutch
cheeses. The following makes a fennel pie:

   Halve 500g/1¼lb fennel bulbs, place
them in a pan, add enough water to cover
and cook for 30 minutes. Drain well. Leave
to cool and then slice.

   Melt 40g/1½oz/3 tbsp butter in a frying
pan, add two sliced leeks and cook over a
low heat, stirring occasionally, for 5 minutes,
until softened.

   Cover the base of the pastry case with
150g/5oz sliced smoked cheese, and top
with the leek and the fennel.

   Beat three eggs with 150ml/¼ pint/⅔ cup
whipping cream and 150g/5oz/1¼ cups
grated mature (sharp) Gouda cheese in a
bowl and pour the mixture into the pastry
case. Bake as above.

125g/4¼oz/generous 1 cup plain
 (all-purpose) flour
125g/4¼oz/generous 1 cup buckwheat flour
1 sachet easy-blend (rapid-rise)
 dried yeast
500ml/17fl oz/generous 2 cups
 lukewarm milk
1 egg
15ml/1 tbsp sugar
5ml/1 tsp salt
25–40g/1–1½oz/2–3 tbsp butter

Old-fashioned pancakes
Ouderwetse pannenkoeken

Pancakes, in Dutch *pannenkoeken*, appeal to adults and children alike, and every part of the world has its own variations. This easy-to-make pancake was, and is still used as, an ideal main dish for informal parties. It is one of the first recipes that Dutch children learn to make for themselves.

1 Sift both types of flour into a bowl, stir in the yeast and make a well in the centre. Gradually pour the milk in, stirring all the time. Beat the mixture to form a smooth batter. Beat in the egg, then stir in the sugar and salt. Cover and leave to rise for 1 hour.

2 Melt a little butter in a 20cm/8in omelette pan. Stir the batter and pour a ladleful (about 100ml/3½fl oz/scant ½ cup) into the pan, tilting and turning the pan until the base is evenly covered.

3 Cook the batter until the top is dry and covered with small holes. Flip over with a fish slice or metal spatula and cook until the second side is lightly browned.

4 Slide the pancake out of the pan and keep warm. Cook the other pancakes in the same way, adding more butter as required.

5 Serve the pancakes with a topping of your choice, such as melted butter, treacle (molasses), jam or sugar.

Per pancake Energy 179kcal/752kJ; Protein 5.7g; Carbohydrate 30.3g, of which sugars 5.2g; Fat 4.8g, of which saturates 2.5g; Cholesterol 34mg; Calcium 104mg; Fibre 0.8g; Sodium 301mg.

Egg pancakes
Eierpannenkoeken

A quicker, modern and more luxurious way of making pancakes is to use eggs as a raising agent. When adding more milk, these can be baked thinly to serve as a dessert called *flensjes*, eaten with sugar, jam or ice cream.

1 Sift the flour into a bowl and make a well in the centre. Add the eggs, egg yolk and salt, mix the eggs and stir, gradually incorporating the flour.

2 Gradually add half the milk and beat with a hand-held electric mixer to make a smooth thick batter. Gradually stir in the remaining milk. Cover and leave to rest in the refrigerator for 30 minutes.

3 Melt the butter in a 20cm/8in non-stick frying pan, and stir it into the batter.

4 Re-heat the pan and cook the pancakes as described opposite, but without adding any further butter.

Variations
• Cook some thin slices of bacon in a dry frying pan until crisp. Remove from the pan, pour in the batter and return the bacon. Serve with treacle (molasses) or a salad.
• Add apple slices to the batter and serve with brown sugar and ground cinnamon.
• Add slices of cheese to the batter and serve with salad.

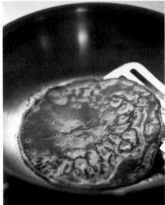

Makes 25

400g/14oz/3¼ cups
   plain (all-purpose) flour
5 eggs
1 egg yolk
5ml/1 tsp salt
750ml/1¼ pints/3 cups milk
25g/1oz/2 tbsp butter

Per pancake Energy 93kcal/392kJ; Protein 3.9g; Carbohydrate 13.8g, of which sugars 1.7g; Fat 2.9g, of which saturates 1.2g; Cholesterol 50mg; Calcium 65mg; Fibre 0.5g; Sodium 112mg.

Beans with pork and nutmeg
Blote billetjes in 't gras

Serves 4

400g/14oz/2 cups dried white
   beans, soaked overnight in
   cold water, and drained
1 bay leaf
800g/3¼lb green runner beans, sliced
200g/7oz lean pork, diced
50g/2oz/⅓ cup diced lean
   smoked bacon
1 onion, chopped
60ml/4 tbsp breadcrumbs
30ml/2 tbsp mild paprika
20g/¾oz/1½ tbsp butter
pinch of freshly grated nutmeg
30ml/2 tbsp cornflour (cornstarch)
1 carrot, thinly sliced
salt and ground black pepper

Variation
Take 250g/9oz white beans, 500g/1¼lb
sliced runner beans and 800g/1¾lb peeled
potatoes. Cook as in the recipe. Mash and
serve with smoked sausage.

Per portion Energy 457kcal/1937kJ; Protein 29.2g;
Carbohydrate 70.1g, of which sugars 9.2g; Fat 8.7g,
of which saturates 3.8g; Cholesterol 17mg;
Calcium 189mg; Fibre 20.1g; Sodium 360mg.

This traditional winter meal was originally made from green beans preserved in salt along with dried white beans. Apparently, the sight of the combination of white and green beans in midwinter used to provoke the wildest fantasies about naked bodies cavorting in spring meadows. As a result the dish was also fondly referred to as "naked bottoms on grass", "naked missies in the green" or "babes in the grass". It is usually served with a sliced warm smoked sausage on top.

1 Put the beans in a pan, add 1.2 litres/2 pints/5 cups water and the bay leaf, bring to the boil and cook for 1 hour, until tender.

2 Cook the green beans in a little boiling water for about 15 minutes, until tender. Drain well, reserving the cooking liquid.

3 Put the pork, bacon and onion in a food processor and process until finely minced (ground). Scrape into a bowl and knead with the breadcrumbs and salt and pepper.

4 Form the mixture into 30 small balls. Spread out the paprika in a dish and roll the balls through it. Flatten them and snip the rims in four places to make "flowers".

5 Melt the butter in a non-stick frying pan. Add the "flowers" and cook over low heat for a few minutes on each side until evenly browned. Remove with a slotted spatula.

6 Drain the white beans, reserving the cooking liquid.

7 Mix both quantities of cooking liquid together, measure and make up to 500ml/17fl oz/generous 2 cups with water, if necessary.

8 Pour the liquid into the frying pan, add the nutmeg, season with salt and bring to the boil over a low heat.

9 Mix the cornflour with 60ml/4 tbsp cold water to a paste in a small bowl and stir into the frying pan. Cook, stirring constantly, until thickened.

10 Ladle some of the sauce into a flameproof dish and add the mixed beans. Top with the "flowers" and garnish them with the carrot. Warm through and serve, handing the remaining sauce separately.

Serves 4

mixed salad leaves
60ml/4 tbsp olive oil
30ml/2 tbsp white wine vinegar
pinch of sugar
500ml/17fl oz/generous 2 cups milk
400g/14oz/3¼ cups grated
    young Gouda cheese
45ml/3 tbsp potato flour
75ml/5 tbsp of Dutch brandy
pinch of freshly grated nutmeg
500g/1¼lb new potatoes,
    boiled and drained
salt and ground black pepper

South Holland cheese dip
Zuid-Hollandse kaasdoop

This dish is a perfect one for children, as the traditional way to eat it is simply to pick up a potato from the pan and dip it into the delicious sauce. To achieve an authentic flavour, you need to use a young farmhouse Gouda cheese made from raw milk.

1 Place the salad leaves in a serving bowl. Whisk together the oil, vinegar and sugar in a small bowl and season to taste with salt and pepper. Set aside until ready to serve.

2 Bring the milk just to the boil in a heavy pan and gradually stir in the cheese. Continue to stir over a very low heat until the cheese has melted.

3 Mix the potato flour with the brandy in a small bowl and stir into the cheese sauce.

4 Cook the sauce, stirring constantly, until it has thickened.

5 Stir in the nutmeg to the sauce and season with pepper. Transfer the pan to a stand over a spirit burner (like a fondue).

6 Pour the dressing over the salad and toss lightly. Put the hot potatoes in a bowl. To eat, spear a potato with a fork and dip it into the cheese sauce. Serve with the salad and more brandy, if you like.

Per portion Energy 701kcal/2920kJ; Protein 33.2g; Carbohydrate 36.7g, of which sugars 9.2g; Fat 44.7g, of which saturates 23.5g; Cholesterol 92mg; Calcium 961mg; Fibre 2.4g; Sodium 996mg.

Five breaks
Vijfschaft

In the 19th century, a lovelorn young man is known to have declared to his sweetheart, "I have been in love with you for years and I am prepared to work five breaks and more, if only I can have you". A normal working day had four breaks – short periods of rest – so the name of this dish implies that eating it will enable you to do more than is strictly required. It comes from Utrecht and if a local wife wanted her husband to do an odd job for her after work, she would serve him Five Breaks.

1 Drain and rinse the beans, place in a pan, cover with cold water and bring to the boil. Lower the heat and cook for 50 minutes.

2 Add the potatoes, onions and carrots, top up the pan with boiling water if necessary to keep the vegetables covered, and cook for about 15 minutes, until just tender.

3 Add the apples and simmer for a further 5 minutes. Drain well, reserving the cooking liquid. Transfer the mixture to a serving dish and keep warm.

4 Mix the cornflour with 30ml/2 tbsp water to a paste in a small bowl, then stir into the reserved cooking liquid. Heat, stirring constantly, until thickened.

5 Stir the butter into the sauce and season to taste with salt and pepper. Pour the sauce into a sauceboat.

6 Cook the bacon in a dry frying pan over a medium heat until crisp. Sprinkle it over the top of the bean mixture and serve immediately with the sauce.

Serves 4

250g/9oz/scant 1½ cups dried
   brown beans, soaked overnight
   in cold water to cover
1kg/2¼lb waxy potatoes, quartered
4 onions, sliced
500g/1¼lb large carrots, sliced
2 tart apples, peeled,
   quartered and cored
15ml/1 tbsp cornflour (cornstarch)
25g/1oz/2 tbsp butter
100g/3¾oz/scant ⅔ cup diced
   smoked bacon
salt and pepper

Per portion Energy 544kcal/2299kJ; Protein 24.1g; Carbohydrate 91.9g, of which sugars 22.9g; Fat 11.5g, of which saturates 5.3g; Cholesterol 27mg; Calcium 131mg; Fibre 17g; Sodium 493mg.

Kale with smoked sausage
Boerenkool met rookworst

Any dish with mashed potatoes and cooked vegetables is a leftover tradition of the "pottage" – vegetables, pulses and meat cooked in one pot – common in the Middle Ages. This was the invention of poverty-stricken housewives who used these ingredients to stretch their limited supplies of meat. This robust fare has developed into the signature dish of the Netherlands. This variety uses kale and smoked sausage.

1 Cook the kale in a little boiling water for 10 minutes, then drain well.

2 Put the potatoes in a large pan and half cover with water. Put the drained kale and the sausage on top, cover and cook over a medium heat for 30 minutes.

3 Remove the sausage and drain the vegetables. Return the vegetables to the pan, mash well and stir in the milk and butter until smooth.

4 Season to taste with salt and serve with the sausage and some butter on top.

Serves 4-5

1.6kg/3½lb curly kale, tough stalks
    removed, finely shredded
1kg/2¼lb potatoes
1 smoked sausage, about 300g/11oz
100ml/3½fl oz/scant ½ cup milk
25g/1oz/2 tbsp butter
salt
butter, to serve

Per portion Energy 452kcal/1894kJ; Protein 14.3g; Carbohydrate 56.2g, of which sugars 20.2g; Fat 20.1g, of which saturates 9.0g; Cholesterol 35.8mg; Calcium 222.6mg; Fibre 9.0g; Sodium 569.4mg.

400g/14oz unsmoked bacon
1kg/2¼lb potatoes, quartered
4 black peppercorns, crushed
800g/1¾lb natural sauerkraut
  (fermented rather than pickled)
1 smoked sausage, about 300 g/11oz
50ml/2fl oz/¼ cup milk
25g/1oz/2 tbsp butter
salt
butter, to serve

Per portion Energy 547.6kcal/2284kJ; Protein
24.5g; Carbohydrate 41.5g, of which sugars 5.9g; Fat
32.5g, of which saturates 13.8g; Cholesterol 77.6mg;
Calcium 137.8mg; Fibre 5.8g; Sodium 2718mg.

Sauerkraut with smoked sausage and bacon
Zuurkool met rookworst en spek

Every Dutch mash is eaten with a well (*kuiltje*) in the middle, in just the
same way it is traditionally served to children. So when presented with a
plate of mash, the diner makes a well, ladles in butter or gravy, and then
spoons up the mash until the dike bursts.

1 Bring a large pan of water to the boil. Add
the bacon and cook for 20 minutes.

2 Add the potatoes, peppercorns, a pinch of
salt and sufficient water to cover. Separate
the strands of sauerkraut with a fork, pile it
on to the potatoes and put the sausage on
top. Simmer gently for 30 minutes.

3 Remove the bacon and sausage. Drain
the vegetables, reserving the cooking liquid,
and return them to the pan.

4 Mash the potatoes and sauerkraut and
add the milk, butter and sufficient cooking
liquid to make a smooth mixture. Serve with
the sausage and bacon on top.

Serves 4

1kg/2¼lb potatoes, quartered
500g1¼lb eating apples, peeled, cored
   and cut into large chunks
250g/9oz cooking apples
40g/1½oz/3 tbsp butter
salt and ground black pepper
fried black pudding (blood sausage) or
   smoked bacon and butter, to serve

Hot lightning
Hete bliksem

This dish takes its name from the piping hot apples. It is made in different
ways throughout the Netherlands. In Groningen (in the north), sweet
apples are used and in Limburg (in the south) the cooked apples and
potatoes are not mashed but simply scooped together. There, the dish
is lovingly called "heaven and earth", or *himmel en eeëd*.

1 Put the potatoes in a large pan, half cover
with water, pile the apples on top and add
25g/1oz/2 tbsp of the butter.

2 Bring the pan to the boil, lower the heat,
cover and simmer for about 30 minutes.

3 Drain well, reserving the cooking liquid.
Mash with the remaining butter, adding
some of the cooking liquid if necessary.
Season the dish to taste with salt and
pepper and then serve with either black
pudding or bacon and butter.

Per portion Energy 315kcal/1334kJ; Protein 4.8g;
Carbohydrate 57g, of which sugars 20g; Fat 9.1g, of
which saturates 5.4g; Cholesterol 21.2mg; Calcium
24.2mg; Fibre 5.5g; Sodium 91.7mg.

Endive mash
Andijviestamppot, broelap, stimpstamp

In the 1930s, cookery teachers used to visit rural areas of the Netherlands to pass on the latest advice about preparing healthy food. This governmental advice was always taken by the locals with a pinch of salt, as these rural communities knew that nothing could be healthier and more nutritious than their mother's potato mash with raw vegetables, or *stamppot met rauwe groenten*.

1 Cook the potatoes in lightly salted boiling water for about 20 minutes, until tender.

2 Meanwhile, cook the bacon, if using, in a dry frying pan over a low heat, turning occasionally, for about 8 minutes, until light brown and crisp. Remove from the pan and crumble.

3 Drain the potatoes, return to the pan and mash with the butter and enough of the milk to make a smooth but not thin purée. Stir in the endive and bacon, if using. Alternatively, stir in the cheese and cook in the microwave for 10 seconds.

4 Serve immediately. All mash is eaten with a well in the centre for a knob (pat) of butter or spoonful of gravy.

Variations
• Curly green endive is a great favourite among the Dutch, but other members of the chicory family, such as frisée and radicchio, are also popularly used as ingredients in this dish.
• Turnip tops (greens), nettles, spinach, purslane and watercress can also served in this way.
• A more recent variation is rocket (arugula) mash.

Serves 4

1kg/2¼lb potatoes
200g/7oz/generous 1 cup diced lean
   smoked bacon or 200g/7oz/1¾ cups
   diced mild Gouda cheese
1kg/2¼lb frisée lettuce, cut into thin
   strips
25g/1oz/2 tbsp butter
100ml/3½fl oz/scant ½ cup milk
salt
butter or gravy, to serve

Per portion Energy 368kcal/1543kJ; Protein 14.6g;
Carbohydrate 48.5g, of which sugars 6.2g; Fat 16g,
of which saturates 7.4g; Cholesterol 41.2mg; Calcium
101.2mg; Fibre 4.7g; Sodium 848.7mg.

Hotch potch with beef
Hutspot met klapstuk

During the Spanish siege of the city of Leyden in 1574, the citizens were so hungry that they were forced to eat rats. When the mayor was implored to surrender the city he replied, "No my friends, rather eat me". This motivated them to struggle on until they were freed by a confederacy of nobles called the Watergeuzen, or "Sea Beggars". Their liberators treated them to a meal of herring and white bread as a reward for their fortitude. Legend has it that they also dined on an *olla podrida*, a stew of highly seasoned meat and vegetables left behind by the fleeing Spaniards. Ever since, Leyden has celebrated this event with herring and white bread and Hotch Potch on 3 October, the anniversary of the liberation.

1 Put the beef in a pan, add the salt and pour in 300ml/½ pint/1¼ cups water. Bring to the boil, then lower the heat, cover and simmer for 2 hours, until tender.

2 Remove the beef. Add the potatoes, carrots and onions and place the beef on top. Cover and simmer for 30 minutes.

3 Pour off the cooking liquid from the vegetables and reserve the liquid. Remove the beef and cut into slices.

4 Mash the vegetables and potatoes, adding a little of the cooking liquid. Season with salt to taste and pile on to plates. Top with the meat and serve immediately.

Serves 4

500g/1¼lb lean boneless beef flank
5ml/1 tsp salt
1kg/2¼lb potatoes, sliced
800g/1¾lb carrots, diced
500g/1¼lb onions, finely chopped

Cook's tip
Make a gravy from the leftover cooking liquid by thickening it with some cornflour.

Per portion Energy 536kcal/2250kJ; Protein 36.2g; Carbohydrate 71.9g, of which sugars 29.3g; Fat 13.4g, of which saturates 5.2g; Cholesterol 73mg; Calcium 122mg; Fibre 10.1g; Sodium 655mg.

Serves 4

500g/1¼lb dried marrowfat peas

For the apple sauce

cooking apples
cinnamon stick
sugar, to taste
dash of lemon juice

For the endive salad

frisée lettuce salad
oil
vinegar

For the other accompaniments,
choose from

crisply fried thin smoked or
        unsmoked bacon slices
small meatballs
fried small pork chops
warm boiled potatoes
golden brown fried onion rings
finely chopped raw onions
mustard
piccalilli
Amsterdam onions and cocktail onions
sweet-sour gherkins

Cook's tip
The main feature of this meal can also be
made with fresh green marrowfat peas,
which need no soaking. Boil them for 15
minutes, or until tender.

Per portion Energy 162kcal/690kJ; Protein 11.6g;
Carbohydrate 27.6g, of which sugars 3.4g; Fat 1.4g,
of which saturates 0.2g; Cholesterol 0mg; Calcium
28mg; Fibre 3.6g; Sodium 680mg.

Captain's dinner
Kapucijnertafel

Kapucijnertafel, or "marrowfat pea table", is the polite name of this dish,
but Dutch people tend to use the sailor's name *Raasdonders*. While some
believe that this name derives from the noise the hard peas make on the
dishes – *raas* means roaring – sailors have a reputation for being coarse
and outspoken. As *donder* is a slang term for the buttocks, the sound in
question is probably something quite different. This masculine dish was
already on the Sunday menu of the Dutch East Indies Company in the
17th century and it is still popular among expatriates.

1 Soak the peas overnight in 2 litres/
3½ pints/8¾ cups cold water. Drain and
rinse well.

2 Put the peas in a pan, add cold water to
cover and bring to the boil. Lower the heat
and cook for 45 minutes, until tender. Drain
and keep warm while you prepare your
chosen accompaniment(s).

3 Finely shred the raw endive and serve
with a dressing of oil and vinegar.

4 To make apple sauce, peel, quarter and
core cooking apples.

5 Place the apples in a pan with a
cinnamon stick, sugar to taste and just
enough water to cover the base of the
pan. You can also add a dash of lemon
juice, if you like.

6 Cook the sauce over a low heat, stirring it
occasionally, until it is pulpy. Then remove
from the heat and cool before serving.

Endive and meatballs
Andijvie zoals thuis

Serves 4

500g/1¼lb lean minced (ground) beef
1 large (US extra large) egg
25g/1oz/½ cup crushed rusks or
   dry breadcrumbs
2.5ml/½ tsp freshly ground nutmeg
2.5ml/½ tsp black pepper
30ml/2 tbsp plain (all-purpose) flour
65g/2½oz/5 tbsp butter, plus extra
   for greasing
pinch of burnt sugar, caramel sugar or
   gravy browning
8 waxy potatoes, halved
1kg/2¼lb frisée lettuce, coarsely sliced
15ml/1 tbsp cornflour (cornstarch)
salt

Cook's tip
You can combine the meatball ingredients
with more breadcrumbs to make the
mixture go further.

Per portion Energy 544kcal/2262kJ; Protein 29.9g;
Carbohydrate 29.3g, of which sugars 2.8g; Fat
36.9g, of which saturates 18.1g; Cholesterol 157mg;
Calcium 96mg; Fibre 3.1g; Sodium 274mg.

Cooked endive is always served with meatballs (*gehaktbal*). The
meatball, once king of pubs and sandwich bars, is the most popular
meat dish in the Netherlands today. Every Wednesday, Dutch
butchers have minced meat on special offer and this is taken full
advantage of by students, who will treat themselves to this traditional
dish when they are feeling homesick.

1 Put the minced beef, egg, crushed rusks,
nutmeg and black pepper and salt in a bowl
and knead until thoroughly combined. Form
the mixture into four smooth balls without
any cracks. Place the flour in a shallow dish
and roll the meatballs through it to coat.

2 Melt 40g/1½oz/3 tbsp of the butter in a
non-stick frying pan. Add the meatballs and
cook them over a medium heat, turning
frequently, for 10 minutes, until browned on
all sides. Carefully pour in 400ml/14fl oz/1⅔
cups water and add the sugar and potatoes.
Lower the heat, cover the pan and simmer
for 20 minutes.

3 Cook the endive in a little boiling water for
10 minutes, then drain well and toss with
the remaining butter. Grease a shallow
heatproof dish with butter and spread out
the endive in the base. Using a slotted
spoon, remove the meatballs and potatoes
from the frying pan. Reserve the cooking
liquid. Put the meatballs in the middle of the
endive, surround them with the potatoes
and sprinkle with nutmeg.

4 Mix the cornflour with 30ml/2 tbsp water
to a paste in a small bowl. Stir into the
cooking liquid and heat, stirring constantly,
until thickened.

5 Ladle a little of the sauce over the meat
balls and pour the rest into a sauceboat.
Serve the endive and meatballs immediately
with the extra sauce.

Variations
• If you prefer a softer, juicier meatball,
use half beef and half pork. Knead with
two slices of white bread that have been
soaked in milk and squeezed out instead
of rusk crumbs.
• The following method shows how the
cooked endive can be mixed with a sauce
instead of simply being tossed in butter:
   Melt 20g/¾oz/1½ tbsp butter in a pan.
Stir in 25g/1oz/¼ cup plain (all-purpose) flour
and cook, stirring constantly, for 2 minutes.
Gradually stir in 200ml/7fl oz/scant 1 cup
warm milk and cook, stirring constantly,
until slightly thickened. Season with salt
and plenty of freshly grated nutmeg.

Meatball and brown bean pie
Filosoof

Serves 4

250g/9oz lean minced (ground) beef
250g/9oz lean minced (ground) pork
1 large (US extra large) egg, lightly
   beaten
25g/1oz/½ cup crushed rusks or dry
   breadcrumbs
2.5ml/½ tsp freshly ground nutmeg
30ml/2 tbsp mild paprika
40g/1½oz/3 tbsp butter
1 onion, chopped
150g/5oz mushrooms
40g/1½oz/⅓ cup plain (all-purpose) flour
50ml/2fl oz/¼ cup Madeira
480g/17oz can brown beans, drained
   and rinsed
30ml/2 tbsp finely chopped fresh parsley
800g/1¾lb waxy potatoes
salt and ground black pepper

For the topping

25g/1oz/2 tbsp butter, melted
30ml/2 tbsp crushed rusks or
   breadcrumbs

To serve

Brussels sprouts sprinkled with toasted
   almonds
apple sauce

Cook's tip

If you would like to break up the method
into stages, the pie can be left to cool at
the end of step 5, and then stored in the
refrigerator overnight.

This pie was originally made of very simple ingredients, mostly leftovers.
So, the crust of breadcrumbs or crushed rusks hides the humble dish
beneath. The Dutch name for this dish is Philosopher, or *Filosoof*, a
reference to what was seen as a philosopher's tendency to disguise
simple truths. This version dates from the 1950s.

1 Put the meat in a bowl with the egg, rusks, nutmeg, ½ tsp black pepper and salt. Knead until thoroughly combined.

2 Form the meat, egg and rusk mixture into about 30 small balls. Spread out the paprika in a dish and roll the meatballs in it to coat.

3 Melt the butter in a large frying pan, add the meatballs and cook over a high heat, stirring and turning frequently, for about 8 minutes, until browned on all sides. Add the onion and mushrooms and cook, stirring frequently, for 2–3 minutes.

4 Sprinkle in the flour and cook, stirring constantly, for 2–3 minutes, until it is lightly coloured.

5 Gradually stir in 400ml/14fl oz/1⅔ cups water, then stir in the Madeira. Season with salt and pepper. Lower the heat, cover and simmer for 10 minutes.

6 Add the beans and transfer the mixture to an ovenproof dish. Sprinkle with the parsley. Preheat the oven to 200°C/400°F/Gas 6.

7 Par-boil the potatoes in boiling water for 5–7 minutes, then drain well.

8 Slice the potatoes and arrange the slices, overlapping slightly, on top of the pie. Drizzle with the melted butter and sprinkle with the pepper, salt and the rusks or breadcrumbs.

9 Bake for 40–45 minutes until golden brown on top. Serve immediately with Brussels sprouts sprinkled with toasted almonds and apple sauce.

Variation

To top the pie with mashed potatoes, cook 800g/1¾lb quartered potatoes in boiling water for about 25 minutes, until tender.

Drain well and pass through a potato ricer or mash thoroughly by hand.

Beat in 2.5ml/½ tsp each salt, paprika and freshly grated nutmeg, 2.5ml/½ tsp ground black pepper, 2 egg yolks and 25g/1oz/2 tbsp butter. Add some milk if the mash seems too thick.

Pipe or spread the mixture over the pie. Sprinkle with rusks and drizzle with melted butter before baking.

Per portion Energy 774kcal/3247kJ; Protein 42.4g; Carbohydrate 77g, of which sugars 9.4g; Fat 33.9g, of which saturates 16g; Cholesterol 161mg; Calcium 185mg; Fibre 11.1g; Sodium 813mg.

Amsterdam beef roll
Amsterdamse rollade

Serves 4

50g/2oz/¼ cup butter
1kg/2¼lb rolled beef, spiced with white
    pepper, freshly grated nutmeg, ground
    mace and ground gloves
1 x 450g/1lb jar Amsterdam onions
    (*Amsterdamse uien*)
300ml/½ pint/1¼ cups red wine or water
15ml/1 tbsp cornflour (cornstarch)
30ml/2 tsp sugar
1.5kg/3¾lb young marrowfat peas, or
    garden peas, shelled weight 500g/1¼lb
100g/3¾oz thinly sliced smoked bacon
800g/1¾lb small potatoes
2 spring onions (scallions), thinly sliced
salt and ground black pepper
apple sauce, to serve

Cook's tip
The Amsterdam onions can be replaced
with large sweet cocktail onions. These
should have a small amount of tumeric
powder or *kurkuma* added (enough so they
look a pale yellow) and should be left in the
refrigerator for 12 hours.

Per portion Energy 913kcal/3813kJ; Protein 74.5g;
Carbohydrate 66.7g, of which sugars 19.8g; Fat
40.4g, of which saturates 18.2g; Cholesterol 185mg;
Calcium 89mg; Fibre 9.5g; Sodium 650mg.

The rollade, or rolled beef, is the Dutch meat of choice for special
occasions. Freshly prepared by the butcher the roll may consist of
beef, veal or pork. This recipe was originally called *rollende*, meaning
rolled loin. The distinctive Amsterdam onions lend a unique taste to
the gravy, hence the name.

1 Start preparing this dish the day before you
intend to serve it. Melt the butter in a
flameproof casserole over a medium heat
until lightly browned. Add the beef and cook
on all sides, including the ends, until browned.
Lower the heat, add 30ml/2 tbsp of the juice
from the onion jar, cover and simmer gently,
turning the beef occasionally, for 2 hours.

2 Transfer the beef to a plate, leave to cool,
then chill in the refrigerator overnight.
Transfer the cooking juices to a bowl, leave
to cool and chill in the refrigerator overnight.

3 The next day, skim off and discard any fat
from the surface of the cooking liquid.
Reserve the solidified frying fat. Remove and
discard the string from the roll of beef. Cut it
into 5mm/¼in thick slices, then reassemble
into a roll shape and tie with kitchen string.

4 Add the wine or water to the cooking
liquid, pour into a large pan and bring to the
boil. Mix the cornflour with 30ml/2 tbsp water
to a paste in a small bowl and stir into the
cooking liquid. Cook, stirring constantly, for 1
minute and season to taste with salt and
pepper. Add the beef to the pan and warm
through over a very low heat for 20 minutes.

5 Heat half the frying fat in a frying pan.
Drain the Amsterdam onions, pat them dry
with kitchen paper and add them to the
pan. Cook over a low heat, stirring
occasionally, for 10 minutes, until they are
evenly browned. Sprinkle with the sugar,
shake the pan well, remove from the heat
and keep warm.

6 Cook the peas in a small pan of boiling
water for 15 minutes. Drain, garnish with
onions and keep warm. Dry-fry the bacon in
a heavy frying pan until crisp. Remove from
the pan and drain on kitchen paper.

7 Cook the potatoes in boiling water for 15
minutes, until tender. Drain well and pat dry
with kitchen paper. Melt the remaining
frying fat in a large frying pan, add the
potatoes and cook, turning frequently, until
browned all over.

8 To serve, remove and discard the kitchen
string. Arrange the meat slices on a shallow
plate. Surround them with onions, potatoes
and peas, garnished with fried bacon. Ladle
some sauce over the meat. Pour the rest in
a sauceboat. Serve immediately with apple
sauce as a side dish.

20 ready-to-eat prunes
100ml/3½fl oz/scant ½ cup brandy
2.5ml/½ tsp grated lemon rind
65g/2½oz/5 tbsp butter
600g/1lb 6oz braising veal, diced
200ml/7fl oz/scant 1 cup veal stock or
    water
30ml/2 tbsp lemon juice
1 thyme sprig
1 bay leaf
200ml/7fl oz/scant 1 cup whipping cream
5ml/1 tsp potato flour or cornflour
    (cornstarch)
salt and ground black pepper
chopped fresh parsley, to garnish

To serve

young peas
carrots
small new potatoes

Maastricht fare
Maastrichtse kost

The people in the southern province of Limburg call themselves
"Burgundians". Many of the French castles still remain – and where you
find castles, you find fine food. Those who worked in the castle kitchens
learned how to prepare sophisticated dishes and passed this knowledge
down through the generations, so the Maastricht cuisine has a quality that
is unsurpassed elsewhere in the Netherlands. Close contact between
Limburg and Germany and Belgium also helped develop new culinary ideas.

1 Put the prunes in a bowl, add the brandy
and lemon rind, cover and soak overnight.

2 Melt the butter in a pan, add the veal and
cook over a medium heat, stirring frequently,
for about 10 minutes, until evenly browned.
Season and add the stock or water, lemon
juice, thyme and bay leaf. Lower the heat,
cover and simmer for 1 hour, until tender.

3 Arrange the vegetables in a ring on a
warm serving plate. Using a slotted spoon,
transfer the veal to the centre of the plate
and keep warm.

4 Bring the cooking liquid to the boil and
reduce slightly, then stir in the cream.
Remove and discard the thyme and bay leaf.
Season the sauce with salt and pepper.

5 Mix the potato flour or cornflour with
15ml/1 tbsp cold water to a paste in a small
bowl and stir into the sauce until thickened
and smooth. Add the prunes with their
soaking liquid and warm through.

6 Pour the sauce over the veal, sprinkle
the vegetables with parsley and serve
immediately.

Per portion Energy 610kcal/2536kJ; Protein 34.4g;
Carbohydrate 19.9g, of which sugars 18.7g; Fat
37.9g, of which saturates 22.4g; Cholesterol 213mg;
Calcium 86mg; Fibre 3.5g; Sodium 286mg.

Mum's braising steak
Lapjes van Moeke

Traditionally, Dutch beef is lean. This is not because of modern concerns about eating too much fat – steak was usually browned in lavish quantities of butter – but because the meat comes from dairy cattle. Green beans are among the most popular vegetables in the Netherlands and, combined with braising steak, they make a classic Sunday dish.

1 Rub the meat all over with salt and pepper. Melt 50g/2oz/4 tbsp of the butter in a frying pan. Add the pieces of steak and cook over medium-low heat for about 5 minutes on each side, until well browned.

2 Add the leek and cook, stirring from time to time, for 2–3 minutes, until softened but not coloured. Stir in 200ml/7fl oz/scant 1 cup water, scraping up the sediment from the pan with a wooden spoon. Add the bay leaf and ground cloves. Lower the heat, cover and simmer gently, turning the meat every 30 minutes, for about 2–3 hours, until tender.

3 Cook the beans in a pan of boiling water for 15 minutes. Drain and place in a serving dish. Toss with the remaining butter, sprinkle with nutmeg and keep warm.

4 If you would like to thicken the gravy, mix the cornflour with 20ml/4 tsp cold water to a paste in a small bowl and then stir into the pan.

5 Transfer the mixture to a warm dish and serve with the beans and potatoes.

Variations
• 7.5ml/1½ tsp vinegar used to be added to the water for braising the steak. Nowadays, red wine often replaces the water.
• For an alternative way to serve the beans, first rinse the cooked beans in a colander. Cook 50g/2oz/⅓ cup finely diced smoked bacon and one small finely chopped onion in a frying pan, stirring occasionally, for 5 minutes. Add the beans to the pan and warm the mixture through.

Serves 4

4 pieces of braising steak, each
   175–225g/6–8oz
75g/3oz/6 tbsp butter
1 leek, sliced
1 bay leaf
pinch of ground cloves
10ml/2 tsp cornflour (cornstarch)
   (optional)
500g/1¼lb green beans
pinch of freshly grated nutmeg
salt and ground black pepper
boiled potatoes sprinkled with
   freshly grated nutmeg, to serve

Per portion Energy 457kcal/1902kJ; Protein 46.8g; Carbohydrate 5.4g, of which sugars 4g; Fat 27.7g, of which saturates 14.7g; Cholesterol 166mg; Calcium 69mg; Fibre 3.7g; Sodium 243mg.

High moorland leg of lamb
Lamsbout van het Drentse Hoogveen

Serves 4

1 leg of lamb, boned with the bones
   reserved
2 egg whites, lightly eaten
7.5ml/1½ tsp yellow mustard seeds,
   marinated in vinegar
50g/2oz/¼ cup butter
sea salt

To coat

2 handfuls of hay
1 handful of heather
cumin seeds
dried camomile flowers
bay berries
dried elderflowers

For the lemon thyme sauce

2 shallots, chopped
1 leek, chopped
6 fresh lemon thyme sprigs
30ml/2 tbsp plain (all-purpose) flour
500ml/17fl oz/generous 2 cups
   gooseberry or white currant wine
heather honey, to taste
full-cream (whole) sheep's milk
   yogurt, to taste
salt and pepper

To serve

Frisée lettuce, thinly shredded
cooked potatoes, thinly sliced
cooked brown beans
crisp smoked bacon
vinaigrette

Cook's tip
This dish can also be served with a salad
of raw chicory (*witloof* or Belgian endive).

Per portion Energy 629kcal/2634kJ; Protein 75.9g;
Carbohydrate 8.5g, of which sugars 2.3g; Fat 23.8g,
of which saturates 9.7g; Cholesterol 265mg;
Calcium 83mg; Fibre 1g; Sodium 219mg.

The Bargerveen is a nature reserve in the province of Drenthe in the north-east of the Netherlands, and the heath there is home to a large herd of sheep, whose meat has a unique flavour. The company who distribute the meat organized a regional recipe competition a few years ago and this is an adaptation of the winning dish by Willem de Witte.

1 Open out the leg of lamb and brush the inside with the beaten egg whites and mustard seeds. Sprinkle with sea salt, roll up and tie with kitchen string.

2 Melt the butter in a large pan or flameproof casserole, add the lamb and cook, turning occasionally, for about 15 minutes, until browned on all sides. Meanwhile, preheat the oven to 150°C/300°F/Gas 2.

3 Mix together the hay, heather, cumin, camomile flowers, bay berries and elderflowers in whatever proportions you like. Remove the lamb from the pan and reserve the frying fat. Coat the lamb in the aromatic hay mixture, then wrap in a rectangle of foil and tie with string. Place the parcel in a roasting pan and roast for an hour, until cooked but still pink in the middle.

4 Meanwhile make the sauce. Heat the pan of reserved frying fat. Add the lamb bone, shallots, leek, lemon thyme and flour and fry, stirring frequently, for 5 minutes.

5 Gradually stir the wine into the pan and bring to the boil, then lower the heat and simmer for 1 hour.

6 Strain the sauce into a clean pan and boil until reduced by half. Season with salt and pepper and stir in honey and yogurt to taste.

7 Remove the lamb from the oven and leave to rest for 15 minutes.

8 Unwrap the lamb and carve it into slices. Serve immediately with the sauce, along with a mixture of endive, bacon, potatoes and brown beans tossed in a vinaigrette and seasoned with salt and pepper.

Leg of lamb with parsley
Lamsbout met peterselie

Serves 4

1kg/2¼lb boned leg of lamb
60ml/4 tbsp finely chopped fresh parsley
2 shallots, finely chopped
1 cauliflower, cut into florets
pinch of freshly grated nutmeg
salt

Variation
If you prefer your cauliflower with white sauce, cook it whole, head downwards, in a pan of boiling water for a maximum of 15 minutes. Drain, reserving 120ml/4fl oz/ ½ cup of the cooking liquid. Melt 25g/1oz/ 2 tbsp butter over a low heat. Stir 30ml/ 2 tbsp plain (all-purpose) flour and cook, stirring, for 2 minutes. Gradually stir in 120ml/4fl oz/½ cup milk and the reserved cooking liquid. Cook, stirring constantly, until thickened and smooth. Season with salt, spoon the sauce over the cauliflower and sprinkle with freshly grated nutmeg.

Per portion Energy 500kcal/2088kJ; Protein 54.1g; Carbohydrate 5.3g, of which sugars 4.3g; Fat 29.3g, of which saturates 13.3g; Cholesterol 190mg; Calcium 75mg; Fibre 3.1g; Sodium 231mg.

This dish, dating from 1761, is very typical of traditional Dutch cooking. At that time, the meat would have been roasted on a spit, but here it is cooked in a thoroughly modern way in a roasting bag. It is served with cauliflower, the number one Dutch vegetable. It is also good with crusty bread and a glass of red Côtes du Rhône.

1 Put a wide, flat, ovenproof dish in the oven and preheat to 200°C/400°F/Gas 6.

2 Using a sharp knife, make diamond-shaped incisions into the fat side of the meat. Rub the inside and outside of the lamb with salt. Stuff the bone cavity with the shallots and parsley. Roll up, with the fat on the outside and tie with kitchen string.

3 Put the lamb into a roasting bag and seal loosely. Place the bag on the preheated dish and roast for 45 minutes.

4 Remove the lamb from the oven and increase the temperature to 240°C/ 475°F/Gas 9. Hold the bag over a bowl to collect the cooking juices and cut off one of the lower corners. Remove and discard the bag.

5 Return the lamb to the dish and roast for a further 15 minutes, until tender but still pink in the middle.

6 Put an ice cube in the cooking juices to help remove the fat, then strain into a sauceboat. Keep warm.

7 Meanwhile, cook the cauliflower in a pan of boiling water for 3–5 minutes, until tender-crisp.

8 Drain the cauliflower well, arrange around the meat and sprinkle with nutmeg. Serve immediately, handing the sauce around separately.

Variation
Other good accompaniments to this dish are the summer vegetables mangetout (snow peas) and baby carrots.

Granny's chicken
Kip van grootje

  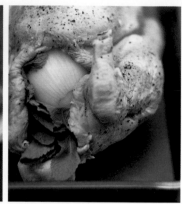

Serves 4

butter, for greasing
1.2kg/2½lb free-range (barnyard) chicken
2 onions
a large bunch of lemon balm, plus
    extra leaves to garnish
800g/1¾lb waxy potatoes, sliced
100g/3¾oz/scant ⅔ cup diced lean
    smoked bacon
salt and pepper

To serve

1kg/2¼lb red cooking pears
½ vanilla pod (bean)
45ml/3 tbsp sugar
dash of red wine
45ml/3 tbsp potato flour

Cook's tip Lemon balm, used here to
stuff the chicken, is easy to grow in a
herb garden. According to the German
medieval abbess Hildegard von Bingen,
the herb is not only tasty but also good
for your nerves.

Per portion Energy 829kcal/3466kJ; Protein 47.4g;
Carbohydrate 79.2g, of which sugars 40.2g; Fat
37.3g, of which saturates 11.1g; Cholesterol 213mg;
Calcium 69mg; Fibre 7.9g; Sodium 573mg.

Many farmers made their living on the fertile soil running alongside the big
rivers of the Netherlands. This dish would have been a typical one in a
farming family, with the wife catching a chicken and her husband
slaughtering it for her. Large free-range chickens were hard to come by
for many years, but now they are once again easy to get hold of.

1 First, make the accompaniments. Peel the
pears, but leave them whole. Remove the
calyx from the base, but leave the stalks.
Place them in a heavy pan with the vanilla
pod and sugar, add water almost to cover and
bring to the boil. Lower the heat, cover and
simmer for 1 hour. Add the wine, re-cover the
pan and simmer for a further 2 hours.

2 Using a slotted spoon, transfer the pears
to a wide dish, standing them upright.
Measure 500ml/17fl oz/generous 2 cups of
the cooking liquid, pour into a clean pan and
bring to the boil.

3 Mix the potato flour with 90ml/6 tbsp cold
water to a paste in a bowl and stir into the
cooking liquid. Cook, stirring, until the liquid
starts to thicken, then remove from the heat.
Pour the sauce over the pears and cool.

4 To cook the chicken, soak a *tontopf* pot
or other unglazed clay pot in cold water for
15 minutes. Dry the inside and grease
generously with butter.

5 Stuff the chicken with the peeled, whole
onion and the lemon balm. Rub the outside
with salt and pepper.

6 Place the chicken in the pot, cover with
the lid and place in the cold oven. Set the
temperature to 240°C/475°F/Gas 9 and cook
for 30 minutes.

7 Meanwhile, chop the remaining onion and
season the potato slices with salt and pepper.

8 Remove the pot from the oven and
arrange the potato slices around the chicken.
Sprinkle the diced bacon and chopped onion
on top.

9 Cover the pot and return to the oven for
45 minutes. Remove the lid from the pot
and cook the chicken for a further 5–10
minutes, until browned.

10 Garnish with lemon balm leaves and
serve the chicken straight from the pot,
handing the pears around separately.

Chicken pie
Kiekenpastey

This chicken pie was traditionally a sweet pie containing ginger, cinnamon, saffron and plenty of sugar. Later, the ingredients included cocks' combs, sweetbreads and chestnuts in an open pastry case. This recipe has been adapted for the modern kitchen and is served as a special treat at Easter.

Serves 6

375g/13oz/3¼ cups strong white bread
   flour, plus extra for dusting
1 sachet easy-blend (rapid-rise)
   dried yeast
150ml/¼ pint/⅔ cup lukewarm water
2.5ml/½ tsp sugar
1 egg, lightly beaten
50g/2oz/¼ cup butter, softened, plus
   extra for greasing
5ml/1 tsp salt

For the filling

1 chicken, about 800g/1¾lb
15ml/1 tbsp lemon juice
50g/2oz/¼ cup butter
150g/5oz minced (ground) veal
pinch of freshly grated nutmeg
300g/11oz pork sausage
150g/5oz oyster mushrooms, diced
8 canned artichoke bottoms, drained
60ml/4 tbsp breadcrumbs
5 small (US medium) eggs
60ml/4 tbsp chopped celery leaves
2 spring onions (scallions),
   finely chopped
100ml/3½fl oz/scant ½ cup
   whipping cream
milk, for glazing
salt and ground black pepper

For the sauce

250ml/8fl oz/1 cup whipping cream
15ml/1 tbsp cornflour (cornstarch)
30ml/2 tbsp chopped fresh chives

To serve

dressed round (butterhead) lettuce

Variation
For a more authentic version of this dish, use 150g/5oz morels instead of oyster mushrooms.

Per portion Energy 982kcal/4093kJ; Protein 39.4g; Carbohydrate 65.3g, of which sugars 3.8g; Fat 64.3g, of which saturates 32.1g; Cholesterol 245.5mg; Calcium 184.8mg; Fibre 3.1g; Sodium 699.8mg.

1 To make the dough, sift the flour into a bowl and make a well in the centre. Add the yeast and water to the well and mix gently, gradually incorporating some of the flour. Stir in the sugar, cover with a clean dish towel and leave to rise for 15 minutes.

2 Add the egg and butter and knead. Add the salt and, if necessary, a little more lukewarm water or flour. Turn out the dough on to a lightly floured surface and knead until it is smooth and elastic and does not stick to your hands. Shape into a ball, return to a clean bowl, cover with a dampened dish towel and leave to rise at room temperature for about 1½ hours, until doubled in volume.

3 Make the filling. Cut the chicken into eight pieces and rub them with the lemon juice and salt and pepper. Melt the butter in a flameproof casserole over a high heat. Add the chicken, in batches if necessary, and cook, turning frequently, for 10 minutes, until browned. Transfer the chicken to a plate and remove the casserole from the heat.

4 Mix the minced veal with the nutmeg, season and form the mixture into small meatballs. Return the casserole to the heat, add the meatballs and sausage and cook, turning frequently, for 10 minutes, until browned all over. Return the chicken to the casserole, cover and simmer for 25 minutes.

5 Remove the meat and leave to cool. Reduce the cooking liquid until it sizzles. Add the mushrooms, and cook for 4–5 minutes. Using a slotted spoon, remove them from the casserole. Discard the fat.

6 Cut the chicken meat from the bones and dice neatly. Thickly slice the sausage. Pat the artichoke bottoms dry with kitchen paper and stuff with the mushrooms.

7 Preheat the oven to 200°C/400°F/Gas 6. Grease a 25cm/10in round non-stick springform cake tin (pan) with butter. Cut off one-third of the dough, knead it again on a lightly floured surface and form into a ball. Return it to the covered bowl and set aside. Knead the larger piece and form into a ball.

8 Roll out the larger dough ball to a 35cm/14in round. Line the prepared tin, gently pressing it on the base and sides; the dough may hang over the rim. Roll out the smaller ball to a 25cm/10in round. Using a heart-shaped cutter, stamp out six hearts.

9 Sprinkle the breadcrumbs over the base of the pastry case (pie shell) and place the filled artichoke bottoms on top. Spoon the diced chicken, meatballs and sausage slices in between the artichoke hearts.

10 Using the back of a spoon, make five hollows in the filling and break the eggs into them. Season, sprinkle with the celery and spring onions and pour in the cream.

11 Cover the filling with the remaining dough, pressing the edges together on the rim. Cut off the surplus dough. Brush the pie top with milk. Arrange the dough hearts and brush with milk. Bake for 1 hour. Halfway through, spray the pie with water and cover the pie with a piece of baking parchment.

12 For the sauce, heat the cream in a small pan. Mix the cornflour with 30ml/2 tbsp water to a paste in a small bowl, then stir into the cream. Season to taste and stir in the chives. Pour the sauce into a sauceboat.

13 Carefully remove the pie from the tin and place on a warm platter. Cut into slices with a very sharp knife and serve with the sauce and a bowl of dressed lettuce.

Guelders goose board
Gelders ganzenbord

Serves 4

4 goose legs, halved
75ml/5 tbsp brandy
30ml/2 tbsp lemon juice
5ml/1 tsp grated lemon rind
salt and ground black pepper

For the sauce

30ml/2 tbsp plain (all-purpose) flour
200ml/7fl oz/scant 1 cup chicken stock

To serve

12 pitted prunes
45ml/3 tbsp brandy
450g/1lb can chestnuts purée
15–30ml/1–2 tbsp whipping cream
400g/14oz Brussels sprouts, trimmed
12 shelled walnuts
salt

Menu suggestion

First course: Queen's Soup
Main course: Guelders Goose Board
Dessert: mature (sharp) Gouda cheese
   then Bavarois with Candied Fruit
Wine: St. Émilion

Per portion Energy 1033kcal/4312kJ; Protein
57.7g; Carbohydrate 62.1g, of which sugars 21.9g;
Fat 55.8g, of which saturates 2.9g; Cholesterol 4mg;
Calcium 135mg; Fibre 11.3g; Sodium 268mg.

In the Netherlands, geese were always raised for the main Christmas dinner, and were especially associated with the province of Guelderland. Those who were too poor would buy a raffle ticket in the local bar or butcher's to try to win a goose. After its slaughter, the bird's head was nailed to the wall and when everyone had eaten the goose, they would call out, "Thank you Mother Goose!"

1 Place the halved goose legs in a non-metallic dish. Mix together the brandy, lemon juice and rind in a bowl, season with pepper and pour over the legs, turning to coat. Cover and marinate in the refrigerator for 12 hours. Meanwhile place the prunes for the accompaniments in a bowl, pour in the brandy and leave to soak.

2 Remove the goose legs from the dish and pat dry with kitchen paper. Reserve the marinade. Rub the legs with salt, and cook in a dry frying pan over a medium heat, turning frequently, for 10 minutes, until browned on all sides. Lower the heat, partially cover the pan and cook for about 2 hours, until the juices run clear when the thickest part of the legs is pierced with the point of a sharp knife. Transfer the goose legs to a plate, cover and keep warm. Reserve the pan of goose fat.

3 To make the garnish, mix the chestnut purée with 15ml/1 tbsp of the reserved goose fat and the cream in a pan and season with salt. Cook over a low heat, stirring frequently, until smooth and warmed through.

4 Meanwhile, cook the Brussels sprouts in a pan of boiling water for 3–5 minutes, until tender crisp. Drain well and keep warm. Drain the prunes, reserving the brandy, and stuff with the walnuts.

5 To make the sauce, drain off all but 60ml/4 tablespoons of the goose fat from the pan. (Store the remainder in the refrigerator for roasting potatoes.)

6 Heat the fat in the pan, stir in the flour and cook, stirring constantly, until lightly browned. Gradually stir in the chicken stock and reserved marinade and simmer gently, stirring frequently, for 10 minutes. Finally, stir in the reserved brandy.

7 To serve the dish, spoon the chestnut purée mixture into a piping (pastry) bag and pipe neat mounds around the rim of a large serving plate. Place the prunes in between the purée and the Brussels sprouts in the middle. Arrange the legs on top and spoon a little of the sauce over them. Serve immediately, with the remaining sauce in a separate dish.

Duck stew from The Hague
Haagse eendenragout

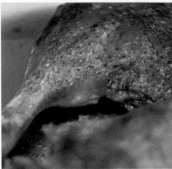

Serves 4

4 duck legs
100g/3¾oz onion, chopped
500ml/17fl oz/generous 2 cups red wine
bouquet garni, consisting of 2 tarragon
   sprigs, 2 parsley sprigs and
   1 thyme sprig
salt and ground black pepper

For the sauce

200g/14oz/3½ cups pitted green olives
200g/14oz leeks, sliced
200g/14oz mushrooms, sliced
2 garlic cloves, finely chopped
25g/1oz/¼ cup plain (all-purpose) flour

To serve

4 slices white bread, cut into triangles
parsley sprigs
tarragon sprigs
a bowl of watercress

Cook's tip
Store any remaining duck fat from this
recipe in the refrigerator and use later for
roasting potatoes.

Per portion Energy 353kcal/1476kJ; Protein 29.7g;
Carbohydrate 9.6g, of which sugars 2.9g; Fat 15g, of
which saturates 2.8g; Cholesterol 151mg; Calcium
78mg; Fibre 3.5g; Sodium 1293mg.

In the 19th century, turbot and duck were commonly available and
therefore inexpensive, unlike today when they are seen as more luxurious
ingredients. A Dutch cookbook of the early 20th century advises the
reader, "Do not always entertain your guests with the same starter,
chicken soup, turbot or braised duck". There are, indeed, many recipes that
use these ingredients that are rather dull and uninspiring. This dish is an
exception, a modern interpretation of a handwritten recipe from the
exercise book of a Hague Cook School pupil of the same period.

1 Tie the legs with kitchen string. Heat a
flameproof casserole without any added fat,
then add the duck legs, skin side down, and
cook over a low heat for about 10 minutes,
until well browned. Turn the legs over and
cook until the other side is well browned.
Drain off and reserve all but about 15ml/
1 tbsp of the fat.

2 Season the duck with salt and pepper, add
the onion and cook, stirring occasionally, for
5 minutes, until softened. Pour in the wine
and add the bouquet garni.

3 Cover and simmer the duck gently for
1¼ hours, until it is tender and cooked
through. Add a little water, if necessary to
prevent the duck from drying out.

4 Remove and discard the bouquet.
Transfer the duck legs to a chopping board
and remove and discard the string. Reserve
the cooking liquid. Cut the meat off the
bones in large pieces.

5 To make the sauce, place the olives in a
small pan of boiling water and cook for 5
minutes, then drain. Heat 15ml/1 tbsp of the
reserved duck fat in a pan. Add the leeks
and mushrooms and cook over a low heat,
stirring occasionally, for 5 minutes, until soft.
Add the garlic and cook for a further minute.

6 Stir in the flour and cook, stirring, for
2 minutes. Gradually, stir in the reserved
cooking liquid. If the sauce seems too thick,
stir in a little water. Add the olives and duck
meat and heat through gently. Transfer the
duck and sauce to a platter and keep warm.
Meanwhile, preheat the grill (broiler).

7 Brush one side of the bread triangles
with a little of reserved duck fat and cook
under the grill until browned. Turn them
over, brush with a little more duck fat and
grill until the second sides are browned.
Arrange them around the stew and garnish
with parsley and tarragon sprigs. Serve
immediately with watercress.

Rabbit in sour sauce
Konijn in 't zuur

Serves 2

150g/5oz pitted prunes
300ml/½ pint/1¼ cups tea
3 onions
40g/1½oz/3 tbsp butter
1 rabbit, cut into pieces, about
    675g/1½lb total weight
100ml/3½fl oz/scant ½ cup red
    wine vinegar
5ml/1 tsp soft dark brown sugar
1 bay leaf
300g/11oz waxy potatoes, diced
300g/11oz tart apples
sugar, to taste
pinch of ground cinnamon
40g/1½oz spice cake, preferably
    Deventer koek
10ml/2 tsp apple spread
30ml/2 tbsp cowberries or cranberries
    (optional)
salt and ground black pepper

Per portion Energy 831kcal/3497kJ; Protein 52.3g;
Carbohydrate 102.3g, of which sugars 70.9g; Fat
26g, of which saturates 14.4g; Cholesterol 217mg;
Calcium 213mg; Fibre 12.7g; Sodium 289mg.

This dish dates from a time when poor people in the province of Limburg would bravely go out rabbit poaching, in spite of the risk of harsh punishment from the landowners. Referred to as *knien in 't zoer* in the Limburg dialect, this is a very old dish, a version of which was first found in a Dutch cookbook published in 1593. The sauce derives its special flavour from the spice cake, *deventer koek*.

1 Put the prunes in a bowl, pour in the tea and leave to soak. Slice two onions into rings and finely chop the third.

2 Melt the butter in a large pan. Add the onion rings and cook over a low heat, stirring occasionally, for about 10 minutes, until lightly browned. Remove from the pan with a slotted spoon and set aside.

3 Increase the heat to medium, add the pieces of rabbit to the pan and cook, turning occasionally, for about 10 minutes, until browned all over.

4 Add the chopped onion to the rabbit, season with salt and pepper and cook for a further 2–3 minutes. Pour in the vinegar and 100ml/3½fl oz/scant ½ cup water and add the brown sugar and bay leaf. Lower the heat, cover and simmer for 1 hour.

5 Meanwhile, cook the potatoes in plenty of boiling water for 10–15 minutes, until tender. Drain well.

6 Peel, core and dice the apples and cook with sugar to taste until soft but not disintegrating. Add the potatoes and warm through.

7 Using a slotted spoon, remove the rabbit from the pan and place on a warm serving plate. Top with the onion rings. Spoon the apple and potato mixture around the meat and surround with the prunes. Sprinkle the potatoes with cinnamon.

8 Crumble the cake into the cooking liquid and whisk until smooth. Whisk in the apple spread. Add the berries, if using, and warm through. Spoon the sauce over the meat and serve immediately.

Jugged hare
Hazenpeper

Serves 4

1.6kg/3½lb hare cut in pieces
300ml/½ pint/1¼ cups red wine or water
50ml/2fl oz/¼ cup red wine vinegar
1 onion, chopped
2 bay leaves
10ml/2 tsp black peppercorns, crushed
40g/1½oz/3 tbsp butter
7.5ml/1½ tsp sugar
40g/1½oz/⅓ cup plain (all-purpose) flour
50ml/2fl oz/¼ cup whipping cream
salt and ground black pepper

To serve

400g/14oz/3¼ cups cowberries or
    cranberries
200g/7oz/1 cup sugar
1 cinnamon stick
Brussels sprouts
knob (pat) of butter
freshly grated nutmeg
mashed potato rosettes

Per portion Energy 997kcal/4199kJ; Protein 89.4g;
Carbohydrate 72.7g, of which sugars 64.7g; Fat
35.4g, of which saturates 8.5g; Cholesterol 22mg;
Calcium 126mg; Fibre 2.1g; Sodium 195mg.

Hunting was always the preserve of the upper classes, and a smallholder or tenant of a rich landowner could risk losing his farm if caught poaching. This simple hare stew would almost certainly have been the result of such a risky enterprise, and would have been cooked with water instead of wine and combined with wild berries.

1 Rinse the hare and rub the pieces all over with salt and pepper. Pour the wine or water and vinegar into a large, non-metallic bowl. Add the onion, bay leaves and peppercorns. Add the hare, turning to coat, cover and leave to marinate in the refrigerator overnight.

2 Remove the pieces of hare from the marinade and pat dry with kitchen paper. Reserve the marinade.

3 Melt the butter in a pan, add the hare and cook over a medium heat, turning often, for about 10 minutes, until lightly browned on all sides. Pour in the marinade, add the sugar and bring to the boil. Lower the heat, cover and simmer for 2 hours, until very tender.

4 Meanwhile, put the berries, sugar and cinnamon stick in a small, heavy pan and cook over a low heat, stirring occasionally, for 10–15 minutes, until thick and pulpy. Remove the cinnamon stick and spoon the mixture into individual pots. Leave to cool.

5 Using a slotted spoon, remove the pieces of hare from the pan and place them on a warm serving dish. Keep warm.

6 Strain the cooking liquid into a clean pan and return it to the heat. Blend the flour with a little water and stir into the liquid. Simmer, stirring constantly, for 3–4 minutes, until thickened.

7 Remove the pan from the heat and stir in the cream. Spoon a little of the sauce over the pieces of hare and pour the remainder into a sauceboat.

8 Cook the Brussels sprouts in a pan of boiling water for 3–5 minutes, until they are tender-crisp (don't overcook). Drain them well, toss lightly with butter and sprinkle with nutmeg.

9 Serve the hare surrounded by potato rosettes and accompanied by the berries, Brussels sprouts and sauce.

Desserts

Sweet things are a real passion with the Dutch and their desserts reveal some delightful examples – included here are the popular children's treat of Poffertjes served with the chocolate drink Fosco, and the glamorous Bavarois with Glacé Fruit.

Porridge, pancakes and poffertjes

Although sugar had been brought to Europe around 350 BC and was much later planted in Spain by the Arabs, sugar cane remained a scarce ingredient in northern Europe. It was available at pharmacies only as a medicine to treat fever and coughs or as a flavouring for the moneyed classes, where it was sprinkled on almost every dish. The "new science" of the 17th century made people believe that fermentation was the driving force of life. As the fermentation of sugar produces alcohol, it was suspected of having dangerous side effects, and so sugar was relegated from the main course to the end of the meal – which hailed the birth of the dessert course, the delicate crown on a fine dinner. Despite this, sweet desserts remained a rarity until beet sugar became readily available in the 19th century.

In the first half of the 20th century most respectable Dutch families had a maid whose task it was to cook the entrée and the main course. The lady of the house restricted her activities in the kitchen to supervision and the preparation of the dessert, the most coveted course. As a result, Dutch families often treasure fine handwritten dessert recipes from their female ancestors that had been enjoyed by the family at the end of a meal. These recipes are often impressively elaborate and the ingredients extensive and rich (one such pudding for four contains 17 eggs). The recipes in this section offer more economical, trimmed-down versions of these luxurious dishes, but still maintain their spirit. For any special Dutch celebration, a handmade dessert will always be chosen to top off the meal over the wealth of ready-made desserts available on the supermarket shelves.

Another sweet Dutch favourite is traditional porridge, made from buttermilk and barley. Semolina porridge with an almond flavouring and rice porridge are other varieties, these both middle-class desserts from the 1950s, a time when Vla (a kind of custard) and yogurt also became fashionable.

Puddings, once eaten exclusively on Sundays, are typically made in earthenware moulds in the shape of rabbits or lambs. Then there is a varied selection of pancakes, *poffertjes*, or fritters, so beloved by the Dutch.

Poffertjes
Poffertjes

 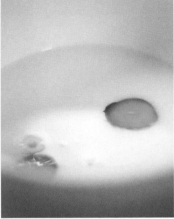 

Makes 72 *poffertjes*; drink serves 6

200g/7oz/1¾ cups plain
(all-purpose) flour
50g/2oz/½ cup buckwheat flour
½ sachet easy-blend (rapid-rise)
dried yeast
300ml/½ pint/1¼ cups lukewarm milk
2 eggs
pinch of salt
25g/1oz/2 tbsp butter, melted

To decorate

butter
icing (confectioners') sugar

Cook's tip

A *poffertjesplaat* pan is the best way to
make these typically Dutch puffs – and are
available at many specialist stores or
internet sites.

Chocolate drink per portion Energy 217kcal/
919kJ; Protein 8.5g; Carbohydrate 36.5g, of which sugars
35.5g; Fat 5.2g, of which saturates 3.2g; Cholesterol
12mg; Calcium 264mg; Fibre 1g; Sodium 167mg.
Poffertjes per item Energy 19kcal/78kJ; Protein
0.6g; Carbohydrate 2.9g, of which sugars 0.2g; Fat
0.6g, of which saturates 0.3g; Cholesterol 6mg;
Calcium 10mg; Fibre 0.1g; Sodium 6mg.

These soft little puffs were a traditional New Year's treat in North Holland,
and were eaten as far back as the 17th century. They used to be popular
with children, and a painting in the Frans Hals Museum in Haarlem shows a
boy stealing one. Many households still own a *poffertjesplaat*, a hotplate
with round cavities. These are traditionally accompanied by a chocolate drink.

1 Sift both types of flour into a bowl and
make a central well. Pour in the yeast and
mix with 15ml/1 tbsp of the milk. Cover with
a dampened towel and stand for 10 minutes.

2 Whisk in half the remaining milk and the
eggs using a hand-held mixer fitted with
dough hooks. Continue mixing until the
batter starts to come away from the bowl.
Whisk in the remaining milk and then the
salt. Cover the bowl with a dampened dish
towel and leave the batter to rise for 1 hour.

3 Heat a *poffertjesplaat*, flat cast-iron griddle
or heavy frying pan over a medium heat.
Brush with melted butter and fill each cavity.
Otherwise, dot the mixture on the griddle or
pan, spaced well apart. Cook until the top is
dry, turn over and cook until no longer sticky.

4 Keep warm while you cook the remaining
puffs in the same way, brushing with more
melted butter as necessary.

5 Serve on warm plates with plenty of
butter, generously sprinkled with icing sugar.

Cold chocolate drink (Fosco)

Use 50g/2oz/½ cup unsweetened cocoa
powder, 150g/5oz/¾ cup sugar, a pinch of
ground cinnamon, plus extra to serve, a
pinch of ground cloves, 200ml/7fl oz/scant
1 cup water, 1.2 litres/2 pints/5 cups milk,
chilled. Mix together the cocoa powder,
sugar, cinnamon and cloves. Stir in a little of
the water to make a thick smooth paste.
Bring the remaining water to the boil, stir it
into the paste and return the mixture to the
pan. Cook, stirring occasionally, for about
20 minutes, until reduced to a light syrup.
Strain, leave to cool, then chill in the
refrigerator. The syrup can be stored in the
refrigerator for up to 2 weeks. To serve,
pour 50ml/2fl oz/¼ cup of the syrup into
each glass and stir in 200ml/7fl oz/scant
1 cup milk. Sprinkle with cinnamon.

Three-in-one-pan
Drie-in-de-pan

Cooking pancakes in a flat pan is depicted in many paintings, from the 16th century onwards. Such works usually show a woman cooking the pancakes, and wearing a scarf to protect her hair from the smoke. This subject became so popular that it was even imitated by Rembrandt. Pancakes usually fill the entire base of the pan, but in his etching three or four smaller pancakes are baked at the same time – as they are here.

1 Sift the flour and salt into a bowl and make a well in the centre. Add the egg and 150ml/¼ pint/⅔ cup of the milk to the well and beat with a hand-held mixer fitted with dough hooks to a smooth batter. Stir in the remaining milk. Stir in the raisins and currants and leave the batter to rest for 30 minutes.

2 Melt a knob (pat) butter in a 20cm/8in non-stick frying pan over a low heat. Using two tablespoons, drop three heaps of batter into the pan and flatten into rounds.

3 Cook the pancakes for about 3 minutes, until the round tops are dry, puffed and full of bubbles. Turn over with a fish slice or metal spatula and cook the other sides for about 1 minute, until browned. Remove from the pan and keep warm while you cook the remaining batter in the same way, adding more butter as required. Serve hot with sugar or jam.

Variation
For an extra fruity texture, add 30ml/2 tbsp finely chopped apple to the batter.

Makes about 12

200g/7oz/1¾ cups self-raising (self-rising) flour
pinch of salt
250ml/8fl oz/1 cup milk
1 large (US extra large) egg
50g/2oz/scant ½ cup raisins
50g/2oz/¼ cup currants
butter, for frying
caster (superfine) sugar or jam, to serve

Per item Energy 208kcal/878kJ; Protein 9.5g; Carbohydrate 28.6g, of which sugars 15.9g; Fat 7.1g, of which saturates 4.2g; Cholesterol 35mg; Calcium 286mg; Fibre 0.7g; Sodium 121mg.

Serves 6

butter, for greasing
breadcrumbs, for sprinkling
125g/4¼oz day-old white bread,
    crusts removed
100g/3¾oz Bitter Cookies or macaroons,
    plus extra to decorate
5 eggs
75g/3oz/scant ½ cup sugar
pinch of grated lemon rind
pinch of ground cinnamon
500ml/17fl oz/generous 2 cups milk
100g/3¾oz/¾ cup raisins in brandy,
    "country lads" (*boerenjongens*),
    drained (see page 21), plus extra
    to decorate

For the vanilla sauce

500ml/17fl oz/generous 2 cups milk
½ vanilla pod (bean), split
pinch of salt
4 egg yolks
40g/1½oz/3 tbsp sugar

Per portion Energy 419kcal/1767kJ; Protein 15.7g;
Carbohydrate 56.8g, of which sugars 39.8g;
Fat 13.7g, of which saturates 5.1g; Cholesterol
303mg; Calcium 298mg; Fibre 0.7g; Sodium 302mg.

Macaroon pudding with vanilla
Bitterkoekjespudding met vanille

With the cultivation of sugar beet in the Netherlands the Dutch developed a very sweet tooth. No meal could be considered finished without a sweet dessert. The Dutch word "pudding" is borrowed from the English, whose experiments with sweet fillings in moulds began the rich history of the sweet pudding in Europe. Here is a Dutch variation on this theme.

1 Grease a heatproof 1-litre/1¾-pint/4-cup mould with a lid with butter and sprinkle with breadcrumbs, tipping out any excess.

2 Cut the bread into wide strips and place in a dish with the cookies. Beat the eggs with the sugar, lemon rind, cinnamon and milk in a bowl and pour a little of this mixture over the cookies and bread. Leave to soak.

3 Make alternating layers of bread, cookies and raisins in the prepared mould, pouring a little of the egg mixture over each layer. Finish with a layer of bread.

4 Close the lid of the mould and steam the pudding in a double boiler for 1½ hours.

5 Meanwhile, make the vanilla sauce. Pour the milk into a pan, add the vanilla pod and salt and bring to the boil. Lower the heat and simmer for 15 minutes.

6 Whisk the egg yolks with the sugar in a bowl, stir in a little of the hot milk, then stir in the remainder. Return to the pan and heat gently, stirring constantly, until thickened. Remove the pan from the heat and discard the vanilla pod.

7 Remove the mould from the double boiler and leave to stand for a few minutes. Take off the lid and invert the pudding on to a serving plate. Pour the warm sauce over the pudding, decorate with cookies and raisins and serve.

Cherry flans
Kersenstruifjes

Serves 2

45ml/3 tbsp sugar
150g/5oz cherries, pitted
butter, for greasing
30ml/2 tbsp plain (all-purpose) flour
pinch of salt
1 egg
15ml/1 tbsp milk
7.5ml/1½ tsp potato flour
15ml/1 tbsp brandy or Kirsch
whipped cream, to serve (optional)

Cook's tip
When served directly from the oven the flans will be beautifully puffed up, and this is the best way to present and serve them. Do not chill them, otherwise they will lose their subtle taste.

Per portion Energy 246kcal/1039kJ; Protein 6g; Carbohydrate 47.1g, of which sugars 32.8g; Fat 3.2g, of which saturates 0.9g; Cholesterol 96mg; Calcium 71mg; Fibre 1.3g; Sodium 41mg.

Dutch cherries are called May cherries, because this is when the trees and orchards are in full blossom. In the cherry-picking season from June to July it is common for people to make special trips to the orchards, sitting on makeshift benches while indulging in the delicious fruit. The idea for these flans comes from an 18th-century recipe.

1 Pour 100ml/3½fl oz/scant ½ cup water into a pan, add 30ml/2 tbsp of the sugar and bring to the boil, stirring until the sugar has dissolved.

2 Add the cherries to the mixture and simmer for 10 minutes. Drain well, reserving the syrup.

3 Preheat the oven to 200°C/400°F/Gas 6. Grease two 10cm/4in non-stick flan tins (pans) with butter.

4 Reserve two cherries for decoration. Divide the remainder between the flan tins.

5 Mix together the remaining sugar, the flour and salt in a bowl. Beat in the egg to make a smooth batter, then stir in the milk. Pour the batter over the cherries and bake for 25 minutes.

6 Bring the reserved syrup to the boil. Mix the potato flour with 15ml/1 tbsp water to a paste, stir into the syrup and immediately remove the pan from the heat. Leave to cool completely, then stir in the brandy or Kirsch.

7 Turn out the flans and serve warm with the cold sauce and the reserved cherries, or cold with the sauce and whipped cream.

Variation
To make a pear flan, halve and core 2 pears and poach in a mixture of 150ml/10 tbsp white wine, sugar and ground cinnamon until tender. Transfer the pear halves to a small ovenproof dish. Boil the cooking liquid until reduced to a syrup and pour it over the pear. Cover the pear halves with two eggs whisked with 60ml/4 tbsp breadcrumbs. Bake in a preheated oven at 200°C/400°F/Gas 6 for 15 minutes. This makes two servings.

Serves 6

8 sponge fingers, about 50g/2oz
100ml/3½fl oz/scant ½ cup Maraschino,
  plus extra for sprinkling
12g/¼oz or 6 gelatine leaves
300ml/½ pint/1¼ cups milk
½ vanilla pod (bean)
2 eggs, separated
75g/3oz/scant ½ cup sugar
65g/2½oz/⅓ cup glacé (candied)
  red and green cherries
25g/1oz/2½ tbsp candied orange peel,
  diced
250ml/8fl oz/1 cup whipping cream

To decorate

120ml/4fl oz/½ cup whipping cream
15ml/1 tbsp caster (superfine) sugar

Bavarois with glacé fruit
Chipolata pudding

A savoury version of this pudding was called "chipolata" in 19th-century cookbooks, a word taken from the French chipolata, a pork sausage. A sweet version for Lent then evolved into this glorious bavarois, created by Parisian chefs who worked for Bavarian princes in the 18th century.

1 Place the sponge fingers side by side on a plate and pour the Maraschino over them. Place the gelatine in a bowl of cold water and leave to soak for 5 minutes.

2 Put the milk and vanilla pod in a pan and bring to the boil. Simmer for a few minutes.

3 Beat the egg yolks with the sugar in a bowl, stir in a little of the hot milk, then the remainder. Return to the pan and cook over a very low heat, stirring constantly, for a few minutes until slightly thickened. Do not allow the mixture to boil or the eggs will curdle.

4 Remove the pan from the heat, squeeze out the gelatine and dissolve it in the warm custard. Remove and discard the vanilla pod. Leave the custard to cool and begin to set.

5 Dice half the cherries. Whisk the egg whites in one bowl. Whip the cream in another. Add the egg whites to the cream, then add the custard, diced cherries and candied peel and fold together. Chill in the refrigerator, stirring occasionally, until thick. Rinse out a 1.2-litre/2-pint/5-cup mould with cold water and leave upside down to drain.

6 Make a layer of the custard mixture in the prepared mould and top with four sponge fingers. Continue making layers until all the ingredients have been used, ending with a layer of the custard. Chill until set.

7 Sprinkle a little Maraschino on to a serving plate and turn out the bavarois. Whip the cream with the sugar. Decorate the dessert with the sweetened cream and remaining cherries.

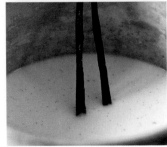

Per portion Energy 332kcal/1388kJ; Protein 7.4g; Carbohydrate 32.5g, of which sugars 30.7g; Fat 20.1g, of which saturates 11.7g; Cholesterol 129mg; Calcium 120mg; Fibre 0.5g; Sodium 78mg.

Heavenly mud
Hemelse modder

This divine mousse, christened "heavenly mud", is a combination of dark chocolate, eggs and cream. It is rich and full of flavour, the height of self-indulgence and a classic sweet in the Netherlands. The ancient Mayan civilization believed that chocolate was the heavenly food of the gods. Similarly, all Dutch people will agree that if the mud in heaven is like the chocolate in *hemelse modder*, it truly is paradise.

1 Put the chocolate and milk in a heatproof bowl and melt over a pan of barely simmering water, stirring until smooth.

2 Beat the egg yolks with the sugar in another bowl. Stir the mixture into the melted chocolate mixture and warm briefly, stirring constantly, until slightly thickened.

3 Whisk the egg whites in a grease-free bowl until they are very stiff. Remove the chocolate mixture from the heat and fold it into the egg whites.

4 Divide the mixture among individual dishes and chill in the refrigerator for at least 1 hour, until set. Decorate with whipped cream and grated chocolate.

Variation
To make another chocolate dessert called Mud from *Gerritje*, substitute icing (confectioners') sugar for the brown sugar and add some vanilla and ground cinnamon to the chopped chocolate. Stir 30ml/2 tbsp brandy into the chocolate mixture just before folding it into the egg whites.

Serves 4

100g/3¾oz dark (bittersweet)
  chocolate, chopped
30ml/2 tbsp milk
4 eggs, separated
25ml/1½ tbsp light brown sugar

To decorate

whipped double (heavy) cream
grated chocolate

Per portion Energy 226kcal/947kJ; Protein 7.8g;
Carbohydrate 22g, of which sugars 21.8g; Fat 12.7g,
of which saturates 5.8g; Cholesterol 192mg;
Calcium 49mg; Fibre 0.6g; Sodium 75mg.

Semolina pudding with redcurrant sauce
Griesmeelpudding met bessensap

Serves 4

800ml/1⅓ pints/3½ cups milk
lemon rind of half a lemon
75g/3oz/½ cup semolina
65g/2½oz/⅓ cup sugar
pinch of salt
1 egg, beaten
15g/½oz/1 tbsp butter
40g/1½oz/⅓ cup coarsely ground almonds
drop of almond extract or bitter almond
  oil, optional

Redcurrant sauce

250ml/8fl oz/1 cup redcurrant juice
1 cinnamon stick
45ml/3 tbsp potato flour
65g/2½oz/⅓ cup sugar, or to taste

Cook's tip
This pudding can be baked in the oven.
Use two eggs and at step 3 whisk the
yolks into the mixture. Fold in the whipped
whites and bake in a greased dish for
25 minutes at 175°C/345°F/Gas 4.

Per portion Energy 398kcal/1679kJ; Protein 12.9g;
Carbohydrate 59.3g, of which sugars 34.1g; Fat
13.9g, of which saturates 4.9g; Cholesterol 67mg;
Calcium 297mg; Fibre 1.2g; Sodium 141mg.

This is one of the simplest of all Dutch puddings, and yet it does need
concentration because if it is overcooked, it becomes really rubbery. To
finish off the pudding, add some butter, an egg and ground almonds, and
serve with the redcurrant sauce recipe described below.

1 Rinse out a heavy pan with cold water,
pour in the milk, add the lemon rind and
bring to the boil.

2 Mix together the semolina, sugar and
salt and sprinkle into the boiling milk,
stirring constantly. Then cook over a low
heat, stirring constantly, for about 5 minutes,
until thickened. Discard the lemon rind.

3 Whisk the egg into the mixture and cook
for a few minutes more. Stir in the butter,
almonds and almond extract, if using, and
remove the pan from the heat.

4 Rinse out a 1-litre/1¾-pint/4-cup mould
with cold water and pour in the semolina
mixture. Leave to cool, then chill in the
refrigerator until set.

5 Meanwhile, make the redcurrant sauce.
Pour the redcurrant juice into a pan, add
250ml/8fl oz/1 cup water and the cinnamon
and bring to the boil. Lower the heat and
simmer for 30 minutes.

6 Mix the potato flour with 90ml/6 tbsp
cold water to a paste in bowl, stir into the
sauce and cook, stirring constantly, until
thickened. Add sugar to taste and remove
from the heat.

7 To serve, turn out the pudding on to a
platter and then pour a little of the sauce
over it. Serve the remainder of the sauce
in a sauceboat.

Variations
• To make an alternative redcurrant sauce,
spoon 450g/1lb of redcurrant jelly or
strained jam into a pan, add the juice of two
lemons and 150ml/¼ pint/⅔ cup boiling
water. Bring to the boil, stirring constantly
and continue to stir until smooth. Remove
the pan from the heat, leave to cool, then
chill in the refrigerator.
• In the province of Brabant a popular sauce
to serve with semolina pudding is made
from blackberries, blackcurrants or
bueberries, simply cooked with sugar to
taste and not thickened with potato flour.

Serves 4

500ml/17fl oz/generous 2 cups milk
1 vanilla pod (bean)
65g/2½oz/⅓ cup short grain rice
pinch of salt
8g, or 4 gelatine leaves
1 egg, separated
65g/2½oz/⅓ cup sugar

Cook's tip
If using canned fruit to decorate the rice pudding, you can thicken the juice by heating it with some potato flour. Leave to cool before serving in a sauceboat, or your pudding will melt when the sauce is added.

Rice pudding
Rijstepudding

Creamy cooked rice (*rijstebrij*) was a classic dish for Sundays, always served with a well of butter and spinkled with sugar and cinnamon. The dish was so popular that it often featured in traditional children's songs. This elegant version is sure to become a family favourite, especially if it is made in a decorative mould. The most popular shape for this recipe is created with a turban-shaped mould.

1 Rinse out a pan with cold water, pour in the milk, add the vanilla pod and bring to the boil.

2 Gradually pour in the rice, with the salt, in a steady stream so that the milk continues to boil. Stir, lower the heat and simmer, stirring occasionally, for about an hour, until the rice is tender.

3 Soak the gelatine leaves in a bowl of cold water. Beat the egg yolk in another bowl. Reserve 5ml/1 tsp of the sugar.

4 Stir the remaining sugar into the cooked rice, then stir in the egg yolk. Remove the pan from the heat.

5 Squeeze out the gelatine and dissolve it in the rice mixture. Remove and discard the vanilla pod. Leave the rice to stand until it is just starting to set.

6 Whisk the egg white with the reserved sugar in a grease-free bowl until very stiff. Fold the egg white into the rice mixture.

7 Rinse out a 750ml/1¼ pint/3 cup mould, spoon in the rice mixture and chill until set.

8 To serve, invert the rice pudding on to a plate. Arrange sliced fruit or apricots in brandy (*boerenmeisjes* or "country girls") on the sides to decorate (see page 21).

Per portion Energy 205kcal/866kJ; Protein 8.8g; Carbohydrate 35.8g, of which sugars 22.9g; Fat 3.6g, of which saturates 1.7g; Cholesterol 55mg; Calcium 169mg; Fibre 0g; Sodium 72mg.

The Hague bluff
Haagse bluf

The ingredients in this fluffy dessert recipe, created in The Hague, are simple and economical, produced out of practically nothing. Before the age of food processors, every Dutch child was happy to beat the mixture for more than half an hour. They knew the reward to come. The bluff is often served with a sponge finger, a wafer or an oblong rusk with a layer of sugar and cinnamon. Here, it is served on a layer of semolina pudding.

1 Bring the milk to the boil in a pan. Mix together the semolina, sugar and salt and pour into milk, whisking constantly. Cook over a low heat, stirring constantly, for 5 minutes, until thickened.

2 Whisk in the egg yolks and cook, stirring constantly, for a few minutes more. Remove the pan from the heat.

3 Rinse a large flat dish with cold water, pour on the semolina mixture and leave to cool.

4 Make the bluff just before serving. First of all whisk together the egg white, redcurrant juice and sugar in a deep bowl until the mixture is very stiff.

5 Then, using a large spoon, make 5cm/2in mounds of the bluff all over the surface of the semolina (one mound is shown below).

6 Touch the bluff lightly with the back of the spoon and raise the spoon to bring the bluff to a peak and make pointed caps. Serve immediately.

Serves 4

500ml/17fl oz/generous 2 cups milk
65g/2½oz/scant ½ cup semolina
pinch of salt
25g/1oz/2 tbsp vanilla sugar
2 egg yolks, lightly beaten

For the bluff

1 egg white
150 ml/¼ pint/⅔ cup redcurrant juice
50g/2oz/¼ cup sugar

Cook's tip
You can buy vanilla sugar at most supermarkets or make your own by storing a vanilla pod (bean) in a jar of caster (superfine) sugar for two weeks.

Per portion Energy 278kcal/1181kJ; Protein 8.4g; Carbohydrate 52.9g, of which sugars 40.3g; Fat 5.2g, of which saturates 2.1g; Cholesterol 108mg; Calcium 188mg; Fibre 0.4g; Sodium 80mg.

Dutch custard
Vla

Serves 4

500ml/17fl oz/generous 2 cups milk,
plus extra to taste
½ vanilla pod (bean)
40g/1½oz/⅓ cup cornflour (cornstarch)
40g/1½oz/scant ¼ cup sugar
2 large (US extra large) egg yolks

Cook's tip
You can use the two left over egg whites
to make meringues (*schuimpjes*) as a
garnish for vla. Heat the oven to
140°C/275°F/Gas 2. Whip the egg whites
until they are very stiff, then add 100g/
3¼oz/scant ½ cup confectioner's sugar and
some vanilla extract. Pipe rosettes onto a
baking tray lined with baking parchment.
Bake them in the oven for 1½ hours until
they have become yellow brown.

This is the most common type of Dutch dessert. Although it bears a close
resemblance to English custard, it is not exactly the same, thickened not
only with eggs, but also with cornflour (cornstarch). Many of the
commercially produced recipes are full of chemical additives and artificial
colours. This recipe provides the authentic flavour of the classic dish.

1 Rinse out a pan with cold water, pour in
400ml/14fl oz/1⅔ cups of the milk, add the
vanilla pod and bring to the boil. Simmer
gently over a low heat for a few minutes.

2 Meanwhile, mix together the cornflour
and sugar in a small bowl, add the egg
yolks and stir until very smooth. Stir in the
remaining milk and strain into a clean bowl.

3 Bring the vanilla-flavoured milk back to the
boil, then remove the pan from heat. Stir the
cornflour mixture into the pan and return to
a very low heat. Cook, stirring frequently,
for 3 minutes.

4 Remove and discard the vanilla pod. Cover
the surface of the vla with cling film (plastic
wrap) to prevent a skin from forming and
leave to cool.

5 Using a hand-held mixer whisk the mixture
with cold milk to create the required
consistency, which is usually a cross between
a sauce and a dessert. Chill before serving.

Variations
• Soak Bitter Cookies (see page 140) in rum
in serving dishes, then cover with vla.
• Heat some vla and melt dark (bittersweet)
chocolate in it. Mix with cold vla and leave
to cool. Serve on slices of spice cake.
• Make the vla as described in the recipe
but mix 50g/2oz/½ cup unsweetened cocoa
powder with 45ml/3 tbsp cornflour
(cornstarch) and 115g/4oz/generous ½ cup
sugar and omit the eggs.
• Ladle vla over any of the following:
strawberries, raspberries, blueberries,
cooked rhubarb or apple sauce.
• To make pears on velvet, mix the vla with
advocaat and serve with halved ripe pears,
covered with redcurrant sauce.
• Mix with the vla with ground cinnamon
and some whipped cream.
• Mix the vla with instant coffee powder
blended with a little water.
• Mix the vla with yogurt, lemon juice and
grated lemon rind.
• Combine several flavours of vla in layers in
a tall glass for a vla flip.

Per portion 163kcal/689kJ; Protein 5.8g;
Carbohydrate 25.5g, of which sugars 16.3g; Fat 5g,
of which saturates 2.1g; Cholesterol 108mg;
Calcium 169mg; Fibre 0g; Sodium 64mg.

Baking

The Dutch diet includes an impressive variety of pastries, cakes and bread – the selection here includes traditional Caramel Waffles oozing with toffee filling, and the self-indulgent breakfast treat of Frisian Sugar Bread.

Pastries, bread, cakes
and cookies

The early Dutch taste for sweet pastries and cakes is illustrated in the 17th-century paintings of Jan Steen, which show Dutch families surrounded by astonishing amounts of cookies and confectionery. This indulgence is also reflected in numerous present-day Dutch expressions. They say *ouwe koek*, or "old cake" when somebody relates a piece of old news, describe a lovely girl as a *snoepje,* or "piece of candy", call a lady past her prime a *heerlijke taart*, or "delicious pie", and describe flattering comments as *zoete broodjes bakken*, or "baking sweet buns".

The Dutch sweet tooth also appears on Koningsdag on 27 April, when the traditional game of *koekhappen* involves jumping up to bite a piece of spice cake that is suspended just out of reach. There is also an immensely popular children's strip by W.G. van der Hulst that revolves around a bakery called *In de Soete Suykerbol*, or "In the Sweet Sugar-puff".

The number of different cookies, often connected with specific cities or regions, is staggering, with the average person apparently devouring no less than 16kg/35lb cookies per head. No wonder, then, that the word "cookie" is derived from the Dutch word *koekje*. Every occasion is celebrated with confectionery: there are wedding cakes, birthday cakes, Christmas rolls and stollen, simnel cakes for Easter and, above all, an abundance of sweet treats on the feast of Saint Nicolas, the Dutch alternative to Santa Claus. Dutch cookies and cakes are often heavily spiced, a heritage of Holland's early access via its colonies to pepper, ginger, cinnamon, cardamon, nutmeg, saffron, clove, citron and orange peel.

In terms of bread, loaves used to be round and shaped by hand, and it was not until the 19th century that these were partly replaced by the loaves baked in a tin (pan) that are common now. So traditional bread was higher and narrower, although any loaves featured in the following selection use contemporary shaped loaf tins. The bread recipes shown here concentrate on special types of Dutch bread that are associated with traditional festive occasions.

125g/4¼oz/generous 1 cup very
    dry blanched almonds
125g/4¼oz/generous 1 cup icing
    (confectioner's) sugar
2 drops of bitter almond oil
50ml/2fl oz/¼ cup egg white,
    lightly beaten

Cook's tip

The Dutch do not like these cookies when
they have dried out and are no longer
chewy. When they reach this stage they
are used in desserts, vla or even cakes.
The cookies can, however, be frozen.

Bitter cookies
Bitterkoekjes

Almonds were widely used during the Lenten fast leading up to Easter,
when all animal foods were forbidden and almond milk was used instead
of cow's milk. Similar in flavour to the crisp Italian amaretti, these cookies
became immensely popular. They differ from macaroons, made solely from
sweet almonds, as they include a proportion of bitter almonds. These can
be difficult to obtain, so bitter almond oil is used here as a substitute.

1 Preheat the oven to 180°C/350°F/Gas 4.
Line a baking sheet with baking parchment.

2 Grind the almonds into an extremely fine
powder in a food mill or an electric grinder,
but do not use a blender.

3 Place the almonds in a bowl, sift in the
sugar, add the oil and mix well. Add enough
egg white, a spoonful at a time, to knead to
a firm dough, then add the remaining egg
white to make a very sticky, flabby dough.

4 Using two teaspoons place 15–18 mounds
of the mixture on the prepared baking sheet,
spacing them apart. Bake for 15–20 minutes,
until lightly browned.

5 Remove the baking sheet from the oven
and leave the cookies to stand for a minute,
then carefully lift the baking parchment with
cookies and place it on a flat surface. Leave
to cool completely before removing them
from the parchment. These can be stored in
an airtight container for up to three days.

Variation

If you use pasteurized egg white, you can
make marzipan, which can be shaped. Follow
the recipe until you have a firm dough (just
before the end of step 3). Shape the marzipan
into seed potatoes, pigs, sausages, carrots
and false teeth, as gifts for Saint Nicholas. You
can also use food colouring in the marzipan,
added at the mixing stage.

Per item Energy 72kcal/303kJ; Protein 1.8g;
Carbohydrate 7.7g, of which sugars 7.6g; Fat 4g,
of which saturates 0.3g; Cholesterol 0mg;
Calcium 21mg; Fibre 0.5g; Sodium 7mg.

Caramel waffles
Goudse stroopwafels

These split waffles with a layer of toffee in between are a speciality of the city of Gouda, but waffle bakers selling them at markets and fairs have ensured country-wide popularity. Their manufacture is now a big industry and you can buy *stroopwafels* in every Dutch supermarket. To make them at home, you will require a round electric waffle iron.

1 Sift the flour into a bowl, stir in the sugar and salt and make a central well. Pour the yeast in and stir in the milk. Cover with a clean dish towel and leave to stand for 10 minutes until the yeast starts to foam.

2 Add the egg and butter and knead until the dough is elastic, adding a little more milk if necessary. Cover with a dampened dish towel and leave to rise for about 1 hour. Shape the dough into 20 balls, cover with a damp towel and leave to stand for at least 15 minutes.

3 To make the filling pour the syrup into a pan, add the butter and cinnamon and simmer, stirring constantly, for 10 minutes. Remove from the heat and cool, then keep it lukewarm in a double boiler. The mixture cannot be boiled again or it will separate.

4 Heat the waffle iron to its highest temperature. If it does not have a non-stick lining, grease it once before cooking the first waffle. Put a dough ball in the iron, press lightly and cook for 1 minute.

5 Remove the waffle from the iron with a knife, place on a board and immediately slice in half with a very sharp and thin serrated knife, starting at the lighter side.

6 Spread the inside of the waffle with a little of the filling and put the two halves back.

7 Using an 8-cm/3¼-in biscuit (cookie) trim the waffle into a perfect round. Make the remaining waffles in the same way. They will keep well for at least 2 weeks in an airtight container.

Makes about 20

250g/9oz/2¼ cups plain (all-purpose) flour
75g/3oz/scant ½ cup caster (superfine) sugar
pinch of salt
1 sachet easy-blend (rapid-rise) dried yeast
25ml/1½ tbsp lukewarm milk
1 small (US medium) egg, beaten
125g/4¼oz/generous ½ cup butter, melted and cooled to lukewarm

For the filling

225g/8oz/⅔ cup golden (light corn) syrup
150g/5oz/10 tbsp butter
10ml/2 tsp ground cinnamon

Per waffle Energy 198kcal/825kJ; Protein 1.7g; Carbohydrate 22.7g, of which sugars 13.1g; Fat 11.8g, of which saturates 7.3g; Cholesterol 39mg; Calcium 27mg; Fibre 0.4g; Sodium 118mg.

Oliebol
Oliebollen

This traditional New Year's treat has outlived all the healthy eating campaigns that tried to limit the number of sweet products in the Dutch diet. Fanatics maintain that if prepared properly *oliebol* or "oil balls" do not contain excessive quantities of oil. In any case, they are far too well established for them to ever be abandoned. Sprinkled with sugar, they are believed to symbolize a sweet and everlasting life.

1 Sift flour into a large bowl and make a well in the centre. Add the yeast and a little of the milk to the well and mix together. Cover with a dampened dish towel and leave to stand for 15 minutes.

2 Stirring from the middle, stir in the remaining milk and the eggs then mix with a hand-held electric mixer with dough hooks.

3 Add the salt to the mixture and continue mixing until the dough is elastic and comes away from the side of the bowl.

4 Mix in all the filling ingredients until evenly combined. Cover and leave to rise at room temperature for 1 hour.

5 Pour the oil for deep-frying into a pan to a depth of at least 10cm/4in and heat to 175°C/347°F. Have two dessertspoons more oil ready in a cup.

6 Scoop a spoonful of batter from the bowl with one spoon and push the batter into the hot oil with the other. Don't add too many balls at once and allow enough room for them to turn over. Cook for 5 minutes, until golden.

7 Remove the balls with a slotted spoon and drain on kitchen paper. Pile the balls into a pyramid on a large plate, wait for them to cool, sprinkle with icing sugar and serve with a bowl of icing sugar.

Makes about 25 balls

500g/1¼lb/5 cups strong
   white bread flour
1 sachet easy-bend (rapid-rise)
   dried yeast
400ml/14fl oz/1⅔ cups lukewarm milk
2 eggs, lightly beaten
7.5ml/1½ tsp salt
vegetable oil, for deep-frying
icing (confectioner's) sugar, to
   decorate and to serve

For the filling

100g/3¾oz/¾ cup raisins
100g/3¾oz/scant ½ cup currants
50g/2oz/½ cup coarsely chopped
   almonds or 50g/2oz/⅓ cup
   diced candied peel
1 tart apple, peeled, cored and
   cut in small cubes

Per item Energy 136kcal/574kJ; Protein 3.5g; Carbohydrate 22.2g, of which sugars 6.9g; Fat 4.3g, of which saturates 0.7g; Cholesterol 16mg; Calcium 60mg; Fibre 1g; Sodium 16mg.

250g/9oz/2¼ cups plain (all-purpose)
  flour, plus extra for dusting
2.5ml/½ tsp salt
90g/3½oz/scant½ oz cold butter
5ml/1 tsp white wine vinegar
500g1¼lb tart apples, such as Goudrenet
  or Granny Smith
45ml/3 tbsp soft brown sugar
5ml/1 tsp ground cinnamon
2.5ml/½ tsp crushed fennel seeds
beaten egg, to glaze
icing (confectioner's) sugar, for
  sprinkling

Apple turnover
Appelflappen

Another sweet product associated with the New Year celebration is
the *appelflap* or "apple turnover". This is a traditional alternative for the
appelbeignet or "apple fritter", which is nowadays preferred by many
because it is baked in the oven rather than fried in oil.

1 Sift the flour and salt into a bowl, coarsely
grate in the butter and rub in with your
fingertips. Using the blade of a knife,
gradually stir in 100ml/3½fl oz/scant
½ cup water and the vinegar. Gather the
dough together and shape into a ball.

2 Roll out the dough on a lightly floured
surface, then fold the top edge down to the
centre and the bottom edge up to the
centre and roll out again to a rectangle. Fold
in three again, cover with clear film (plastic
wrap) and leave to rest in the refrigerator.

3 Peel the apples and grate coarsely into
a bowl. Stir in the sugar, cinnamon and
fennel seeds.

4 Preheat the oven to 200°C/400°F/Gas 6.
Line a 30 x 40-cm/12 x 16-in baking sheet
with baking parchment.

5 Roll out the dough on a lightly floured
surface to 36 x 48-cm/14¼ x 19-in rectangle,
then cut into 12 squares. Cover the centre
of each square with some grated apple and
fold over to make a triangle. Press the
edges together with a fork.

6 Transfer to the prepared baking sheet and
brush with beaten egg. Prick the tops
several times with a fork. Bake for about
35 minutes. Remove from the oven and
leave to cool, then sprinkle generously
with icing sugar.

Per item Energy 156kcal/658kJ; Protein 2.2g;
Carbohydrate 23.9g, of which sugars 8g; Fat 6.5g,
of which saturates 4g; Cholesterol 16mg;
Calcium 34mg; Fibre 1.3g; Sodium 47mg.

St Nicholas slices
Gevulde speculaas

  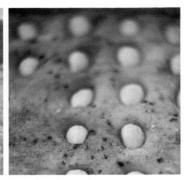

Makes 30-36 pieces

125g/4¼oz/generous ½ cup butter,
   softened, plus extra for greasing
breadcrumbs, for sprinkling
250g/9oz/2¼ cups plain (all-purpose)
   flour, plus extra for dusting
2.5ml/½ tsp baking powder
7.5ml/1½ tsp ground cinnamon
2.5ml/½ tsp ground nutmeg
2.5ml/½ tsp ground cardamom
2.5ml/½ tsp ground allspice
pinch of salt
1.5ml/¼ tsp crushed aniseed
150g/5oz/⅔ cups Muscovado sugar
60ml/4 tbsp milk, plus extra for brushing
400g/14oz almond paste (see cook's tip)
1 small (US medium) egg
50 split blanched almonds, to decorate

Cook's tip

To make almond paste, mix together
200g/7oz/1¾ cups ground almonds, 200g/
7oz/1 cup sugar, 1 small (US medium) egg,
a drop of bitter almond oil or almond
extract and a pinch of grated lemon rind.
Knead until smooth, then wrap and chill in
the refrigerator until ready to use.

Per slice Energy 126kcal/527kJ; Protein 2.2g;
Carbohydrate 16.2g, of which sugars 10.6g; Fat 6.3g,
of which saturates 2.1g; Cholesterol 12.7mg;
Calcium 0.6mg; Fibre 0.6g; Sodium 25mg.

Spicy speculaas is one of the traditional gifts on 5 December, the eve
of the Saint's day of Saint Nicholas. The dough would formerly have been
shaped in artfully carved wooden moulds, representing themes from daily
life, hence the name from the Latin word *speculum*, meaning mirror.
As the dough is nowadays made lighter, most of the forms are gone, with
only the "poppen", dolls, depicting courtship, and the small cookies, mostly
windmills, remaining. The dough is baked as a thick layer and then broken.
Here is the softer filled version, a favourite nowadays.

1 Preheat the oven to 180°C/350°F/Gas 4.
Grease a shallow 23cm/9in square or
17 x 25cm/6½ x 10in rectangular cake tin
(pan) with butter. Sprinkle with breadcrumbs
to coat, shaking out any excess.

2 Sift the flour with the baking powder,
cinnamon, nutmeg, cardamom, allspice and
salt into a bowl. Stir in the aniseed and sugar.

3 Add the butter and cut it into the flour
mixture with two knives. Knead, adding
the milk a spoonful at a time, until the
dough is smooth and elastic. You may not
require all the milk.

4 Halve the dough and form it into two
balls. Roll out one ball on a lightly floured
surface to the same shape as the prepared
tin but slightly larger.

5 Use the dough to line the tin, easing it up
the sides and letting it overhang the rim. Roll
out the second dough ball in the same way.

6 Mix the almond paste with the egg in a
bowl. Spread this over the dough in the tin
with dampened fingers. Cover the paste with
the second piece of dough, pressing the
edges to seal. Trim off any overhanging
dough. Brush the top with milk and decorate
with the almonds in neat rows. Prick little
holes in between the nuts.

7 Bake for 50 minutes, gently flattening any
bubbles with the back of a spoon after 30
minutes. Remove from the oven, cover with
foil and leave to cool in the tin. Cut into
rectangular pieces before serving.

Variations

If you have a wooden *speculaas* mould you
can make dolls from the same dough. Bake
these for about 20 minutes in a preheated
oven at 180°C/250°F/Gas 4. For *pepernoten*
(pepper nuts) hazelnut-size balls are rolled
from the dough and divided over two baking
sheets and baked for about 10 minutes at
180°C/250°F/Gas 4.

500g/1¼lb/5 cups plain (all-purpose)
   flour, plus extra for dusting
1 sachet easy-blend (rapid-rise)
   dried yeast
2.5ml/½ tsp sugar
300ml/½ pint/1¼ cups lukewarm milk
25g/1oz/2 tbsp butter, softened,
   plus extra for greasing
10ml/2 tsp salt
1 egg yolk, beaten with 5ml/1 tsp milk
poppy seeds, sesame seeds, caraway
   seeds, to decorate

The Hague breakfast
Haags ontbijt

These soft buns are delicious at any time of day and are always a big success at children's parties, especially if you allow the children to make them. They are also a good addition at picnics and barbecues and are ideal for a festive breakfast. They can be made well in advance as they freeze well – so it's worth keeping a bag in the freezer for unexpected visitors.

1 Sift the flour into a bowl and make a well in the centre. Add the yeast and sugar to the well and stir in a little of the milk. Leave to stand for 10 minutes.

2 Add the remaining milk and the butter and knead together, then add the salt. Knead well to a smooth elastic dough, adding a little more milk if necessary. Cover with a dampened dish towel and leave to rise at room temperature for about 1 hour, until doubled in bulk.

3 Turn out the dough on to a lightly floured surface and press out into a square, then cut into 40 equal pieces. Cover them with a damp dish towel.

4 Working on one piece of dough at a time, roll into thin strips on a dampened surface.

5 Form the strips into shapes such as knots, snails, figures of eight, pretzels and plaits (braids). Cover with a dampened dish towel and leave to rise for 30 minutes.

6 Preheat the oven to 220°C/425°F/Gas 7. Grease a baking sheet with butter.

7 Transfer the shapes to the prepared baking sheet, brush with the egg yolk and milk and sprinkle some with poppy seeds, some with sesame seeds and others with caraway seeds. Bake for 15–20 minutes, until golden brown.

Per bun Energy 53kcal/222kJ; Protein 1.5g; Carbohydrate 10.1g, of which sugars 0.6g; Fat 0.9g, of which saturates 0.5g; Cholesterol 7mg; Calcium 27mg; Fibre 0.4g; Sodium 8mg.

John Hail cookie
Janhagel

This cookie was a kind of flat, leathery, chewy treat, consisting of small drops of dough baked together. *Janhagel* was used as a term for "ragtag and bobtail" and the cookie owed its name to the fact that it was sold to people who could not afford more sophisticated baked goods. However, in the 19th century, the name inspired an inventive baker to provide the cookie with a layer that resembled *hagel*, or "hail". Combined with *Jan,* a common Dutch forename, the result was an irresistible sweet.

Makes about 32

150g/5oz/10 tbsp butter, plus extra
   for greasing
breadcrumbs, for sprinkling (optional)
250g/9oz/2¼ cups plain (all-purpose)
   flour, plus extra for dusting
75g/3oz/scant ½ cup caster sugar
75g/3oz/⅓ cup Muscovado sugar
2.5ml/½ tsp tartaric acid
1.5ml/¼ tsp bicarbonate of soda
   (baking soda)
2.5ml/½ tsp vanilla seeds
2.5ml/½ tsp aniseed
2.5ml/½ tsp ground cinnamon
1 egg

To decorate

45ml/3 tbsp flaked (sliced) almond
45ml/3 tbsp small pearl sugar

Cook's tip

In the Netherlands, pearl sugar, or *greinsuikerklontjes* is only available at the baker's. You could also use normal sugar cubes crushed into grains with a dough roll, and then sieve the finer grains out.

1 Preheat the oven to 160°C/325°F/Gas 3. Grease a 40 x 35cm/16 x 14in baking sheet with butter and sprinkle with breadcrumbs or line with baking parchment.

2 Sift the flour, sugar, tartaric acid and soda into a bowl. Stir in the vanilla seeds, aniseed and cinnamon. Add the egg, then add the butter. Cut with two knives into very small lumps, then knead an elastic dough.

3 With floured fingers, press the dough on to the baking sheet, spreading it out to within 2cm/¾in of the rim.

4 Sprinkle with the almonds and *greinsuikerklontjes*, pressing them in well.

5 Bake for 25–30 minutes, until golden brown. Remove the baking sheet from the oven and cut the pastry into bars.

6 Using a spatula, transfer them to a flat, dry surface to cool. If the undersides of the bars are still soft and pale, turn them upside down on the baking sheet and return to the oven for a few minutes. These can be stored for several weeks in an airtight container.

Per cookie Energy 96kcal/400kJ; Protein 1.2g; Carbohydrate 12.7g, of which sugars 6.6g; Fat 4.8g, of which saturates 2.5g; Cholesterol 10mg; Calcium 19mg; Fibre 0.3g; Sodium 29mg.

Dutch apple pie
Hollandse appeltaart

Makes one 33cm/13in pie

175g/6oz/¾ cup butter, softened,
  plus extra for greasing
175g/6oz/1½ cups plain (all-purpose)
  flour, plus extra for dusting
175g/6oz/1½ cups self-raising
  (self-rising) flour
175g/6oz/scant 1 cup caster
  (superfine) sugar
1 egg
2.5ml/½ teaspoon grated lemon rind
pinch of salt

For the filling

1kg/2¼lb tart apples, such as Goudrenet
  or Granny Smith
juice of 1 lemon
60ml/4 tbsp sugar
10ml/2 tsp ground cinnamon
30ml/2 tbsp breadcrumbs
5ml/1 tsp aniseed, crushed

For the glaze

60ml/4 tbsp apricot jam
30ml/2 tbsp rum

Per pie Energy 4174kcal/17592kJ; Protein 48.1g;
Carbohydrate 672.4g, of which sugars 383.2g;
Fat 155.5g, of which saturates 93.4g; Cholesterol
563mg; Calcium 760mg; Fibre 27.5g; Sodium 1431mg.

The national sweet pastry of the Netherlands is apple pie. Early recipes, dating from the Middle Ages, instructed the cook to sprinkle a lot of spices, such as cardamom, ginger, cloves, mace, and cinnamon, over "golden apples" and the cooking time was measured in the number of paternosters, or prayers, you had to say. Consequently, the outcome was unpredictable. The invention of the oven with heat controls solved this problem. Nowadays, apple pie is displayed in show-cases on bars in cafés and coffee shops. The first cake a Dutch child learns to bake is an apple pie, still best made with the Goudrenet variety.

1 Preheat the oven to 200°C/400°F/Gas 6. Then grease a 33cm/13in springform tin (pan) with butter.

2 To make the filling, peel, core and thinly slice the apples, then place them in a non-metallic bowl.

3 Mix together the lemon juice, sugar and cinnamon, pour over the apples and set aside.

4 Meanwhile, make the dough. Sift the flour into a bowl and stir in the sugar. butter, egg, lemon rind and salt and knead to a dough. Cut off one-third of the dough and set aside.

5 Roll out the remaining dough on a lightly floured surface to a 37cm/14½in round and use to line the prepared tin. If the dough cracks, press it gently together again.

6 Mix together the breadcrumbs and aniseed and sprinkle the mixture evenly over the base of the pastry case (pie shell). Arrange the apple slices in slightly overlapping concentric circles on top.

7 Roll out the remaining dough to a 33cm/13in round. Cut into 1-cm/½-in wide strips and arrange them in a lattice pattern over the apples.

8 Bake for 45–55 minutes, until golden brown. Meanwhile, mix together the jam and rum for the glaze.

9 Remove the pie from the oven and, while still warm, brush the top with the glaze. Carefully lift off the sides of the tin, place a cake dome or upturned bowl over the pie and leave to cool. This pie freezes well.

Limburg tart
Limburgse vlaai

Serves 6–8

300g/11oz/2¾ cups plain (all-purpose)
    flour, plus extra for dusting
½ sachet easy-blend (rapid-rise)
    dried yeast
5ml/1 tsp sugar
100ml/3½fl oz/scant ½ cup lukewarm milk
25g/1oz/2 tbsp butter, softened, plus
    extra for greasing
25g/1oz/2 tbsp caster (superfine) sugar
1 egg, beaten
5ml/1 tsp salt

For the filling

250ml/9fl oz/generous 1 cup milk
¼ vanilla pod (bean)
2 egg yolks
50g/2oz/¼ cup caster (superfine) sugar
25g/1oz/¼ cup cornflour (cornstarch)

For the topping

500–800g/1¼–1¾lb bottled, canned or
    prepared fresh fruit, such as sliced
    apples, halved plums, halved apricots
    or cherries (do not use berries)
50g/2oz/¼ cup sugar (optional)

To decorate

150ml/¼ pint/⅔ cup juice
15ml/1 tbsp potato flour
or sugar

Cook's tip
For an authentic *vlaai*, always use one kind
of fruit and ensure that the rim of the
dough is not higher than 3cm (1¼in). It has
to be a flat tart, as the name is derived
from the Latin word *platus*, meaning flat.

Per portion Energy 265kcal/1123kJ; Protein 6g;
Carbohydrate 51.6g, of which sugars 20.2g; Fat
5.3g, of which saturates 2.6g; Cholesterol 59.6mg;
Calcium 123mg; Fibre 2.2g; Sodium 46mg.

This sweet tart from the south of the Netherlands boasts a long history.
There are records of the word *vladbecker*, meaning "baker of flat tarts,"
going back to 1338. In Limburg the tart was originally a special treat during
a twice yearly church fair. Now it is available widely throughout the country.

1 Sift the flour and make a well. Pour the
yeast into the well and add the sugar and
a little of the milk. Leave for 10 minutes.
Add the remaining milk, the butter, sugar
and egg, knead well, then add the salt.

2 Knead well until the dough is no longer
sticky and small holes have formed that
burst when you squeeze them. If the dough
seems too dry, add some extra milk.

3 Cover the bowl with a dampened dish
towel and leave the dough to stand at room
temperature until it has doubled in size.

4 Preheat the oven to 200°C/400°F/Gas 6.
Then grease a 30cm/12in flan tin (pan)
with butter. Roll out the dough to a round on
a lightly floured surface. Line the prepared
tin with the dough round so that it comes
about 3cm/1¼in up the side. Prick the base
with a fork, cover with dampened dish towel
and leave to rise for about 15 minutes.

5 Make the filling of the tart. Pour 200ml/
7fl oz/scant 1 cup of the milk into a pan,
then add the vanilla pod and heat gently.

6 Beat the yolks with the sugar and cornflour
in a bowl, then stir in the remaining milk and
strain into a jug (pitcher). Gradually stir the
egg yolk mixture into the vanilla-flavoured
milk, then continue to cook, stirring
constantly, for a few minutes, until thickened.

7 Remove the pan from the heat, cover the
surface with clear film (plastic wrap) to
prevent a skin forming and leave until
lukewarm. Discard the vanilla pod. Whisk the
filling until creamy.

8 Drain the canned fruit, if using, and reserve
150ml/¼ pint/⅔ cup of the juice. Heat the
juice in a pan. Mix the potato flour with
30ml/2 tbsp water to a paste in a bowl, then
stir into the juice and cook, stirring until
thickened. Remove from the heat and cool.

9 Spread the filling over base of the pastry
case (pie shell) and cover with the fruit. If
using plums or apricots, place them cut
side up. Sprinkle the fresh fruit with sugar.
Bake for 30–35 minutes. Remove from the
oven and leave to cool. Decorate with the
thickened juice or sprinkle with sugar.

Frisian sugar bread
Suikerbrood

Makes 1 loaf

500g/1¼lb/5 cups strong white bread
   flour, plus extra for dusting
2 sachets easy-blend (rapid-rise)
   dried yeast
300ml/½ pint/1¼ cups lukewarm milk
50g/2oz/¼ cup caster (superfine) sugar
pinch of ground cinnamon
pinch of ground nutmeg
pinch of powdered saffron
50g/2oz/¼ cup butter, softened,
   plus extra for greasing
1 egg yolk
10ml/2 tsp salt
sugar, for sprinkling

For the filling

250g/9oz pearl sugar, or hazelnut size
   pearl sugar, or *grove greinsuiker*
5ml/1 tsp cinnamon

Cook's tip
If you don't have pearl sugar (*grove
greinsuiker*) use small sugar cubes or
white cane sugar lumps.

Per loaf Energy 3458kcal/14660kJ; Protein 61.9g;
Carbohydrate 716.4g, of which sugars 335.4g; Fat
58.2g, of which saturates 31.8g; Cholesterol 326mg;
Calcium 1251mg; Fibre 15.5g; Sodium 474mg.

An excerpt from a 17th-century sermon said that, "…were they not ashamed to do so, men would found an academy to which they would send all cooks and pastry bakers". Such sermons did not dampen the Dutch passion for sweets, and they still indulge their sweet tooth at breakfast. The ultimate delight is this Frisian speciality, now sold all over the country.

1 Sift the flour into a bowl and make a well in the centre. Add the yeast and a little milk and mix to a creamy consistency, incorporating some of the flour. Add 5ml/ 1 tsp of the sugar. Cover with a clean dish towel and leave to stand for 10 minutes.

2 Add the cinnamon, nutmeg and saffron to the remaining milk, add to the bowl and mix. Add the egg yolk, the remaining sugar and the butter and knead briefly, then add the salt. Turn out on to a lightly floured surface and knead vigorously for at least 15 minutes, until the dough is no longer sticky and is full of little bubbles. Add extra milk if necessary.

3 Form the dough into a ball, return to a clean bowl and cover with a dampened dish towel. Leave to stand at room temperature for 1 hour, or until it has doubled in bulk.

4 Toss the pearl sugar with the cinnamon in a bowl, then flour your hands and knead the grains into the dough.

5 Turn out the dough on to a lightly floured surface and push it out into a rectangle 30cm/12in wide. Brush the flour away on both sides. Roll up the rectangle, starting at the top or bottom, wherever the filling is most sparse.

6 Grease a 2-litre (3½-pint) rectangular loaf tin (pan) with butter and sprinkle with sugar. Put the dough roll into the tin, with the final fold underneath. Cover the tin with a dampened dish towel and leave to stand at room temperature for about 1 hour, until the dough has just risen above the rim.

7 Preheat the oven to 200°C/400°F/Gas 6. To prevent the sugar from dripping into the oven, it is advisable to place a sheet of baking parchment underneath the tin.

8 Bake for 30 minutes. If the top seems to be browning too quickly, cover it with foil after 20 minutes. Brush the top of the loaf with cold water and return it the oven for 1 minute. Turn out the loaf on to a wire rack and leave to cool.

Spice cake
Koek

Any Dutch traveller visiting a Middle Eastern market immediately feels at home as the aroma of coffee and spices reminds them of their familiar snack of coffee and spiced cake. For centuries the spice route ran overland, but the sea route provided the Dutch with easier access to spices. This wheat flour and sugar recipe dates from World War II when traditional spice cakes, made from rye flour and honey, were not available.

1 Preheat the oven to 150°C/300°F/Gas 2. Using a 2 litre (4¼ pint) volume cake tin (pan) grease the cake tin with butter, sprinkle with breadcrumbs and shake out any excess.

2 Sift the flour, baking powder and salt into a large bowl and stir in the sugar, cinnamon, allspice, cloves, nutmeg and cardamom, taking care to break up any sugar lumps.

3 Gradually stir in the milk to the mixture, then whisk until the mixture is smooth with a dropping (pourable) consistency.

4 Pour the mixture into the prepared tin and bake for 1½ hours, or until a wooden cocktail stick (toothpick) inserted in the centre comes out clean.

5 Remove from the oven, turn out on to a wire rack and leave to cool.

6 Wrap the cake in foil and store for at least 3 days before eating to allow the flavour of the spices to develop fully.

Serves 20

butter, for greasing
breadcrumbs, for sprinkling
500g/1¼lb/5 cups plain (all-purpose) flour
20ml/4 tsp baking powder
5ml/1 tsp salt
350g12oz/1½ cups Muscovado sugar
10ml/2 tsp ground cinnamon
1.5ml/¼ tsp ground allspice
1.5ml/¼ tsp ground cloves
2.5ml/½ tsp ground nutmeg
1.5ml/¼ tsp ground cardamom
400–450ml/14–15 fl oz/1⅔–2 cups milk

Cook's tip
In a rectangular form, this kind of cake is often served well buttered at breakfast (the Dutch always use a rectangular cake tin).

Per portion Energy 166.5kcal/708kJ; Protein 3.2g; Carbohydrate 39.2g, of which sugars 19.6g; Fat 0.7g, of which saturates 0.3g; Cholesterol 1.2mg; Calcium 80mg; Fibre 0.7g; Sodium 227mg.

Dutch wholemeal bread
Hollands volkorenbrood

Every country has its own favourite types of bread. The Dutch share their preference for loaves baked in a tin with the English, although the shape and ingredients inevitably differ. This recipe is a traditional one for a true Dutch wholemeal loaf.

1 For the starter, mix together the flour and yeast in a large measuring jug (cup) of 1 litre and stir in the water, a spoonful at a time, until creamy. Cover with foil and leave to stand until the mixture has foamed up to measure 1 litre/1¾ pints/4 cups.

2 Put the flour, sugar and butter in the bowl of an electric mixer. Add the starter and the lukewarm water and knead slowly with the mixer fitted with a dough hook. Add the salt after a few minutes, then increase the speed of the mixer and knead for about 15 minutes, until the dough comes away from the side of the bowl.

3 Transfer the dough to a very large bowl (4.5 litres/8 pints/4¾ quarts). Cover with damp muslin (cheesecloth) and leave to stand until the dough has risen just above the bowl rim.

4 Preheat the oven to 220°C/425°F/Gas 7. Brush two 30 x 10 x 10-cm/12 x 10 x 10-in loaf tins (pans), with melted butter.

5 Turn out the dough on to a lightly floured surface and with floured hands shape it into a rectangle 30cm/12in wide. Using kitchen scissors, cut the rectangle in half widthways. Dust both pieces of dough with flour and brush off any excess. Roll up both rectangles and place in the prepared tins, with the folds underneath. Cover with dampened muslin and leave until the dough has risen well above the rims of the tins.

6 Bake for 20–25 minutes, but do not allow the crusts to become too dark. Brush the tops of the loaves with cold water and return to the oven for 1 minute. Turn out the loaves on to wire racks and leave to cool.

Makes 2 loaves

800g/1¾lb/7 cups wholemeal (whole-wheat) flour, plus extra for dusting
40g/1½oz/3 tbsp golden caster (superfine) sugar
40g/1½oz/3 tbsp butter, softened
450ml/¾ pint/scant 2 cups lukewarm water
25ml/1½ tbsp salt
melted butter, for brushing

For the starter

200g/7oz/1¾ cups wholemeal (whole-wheat) flour
3 sachets easy-blend (rapid-rise) dried yeast
200–300ml/7–10fl oz/scant 1–1¼ cups lukewarm water

Per loaf Energy 1933kcal/8198kJ; Protein 47.2g; Carbohydrate 409.5g, of which sugars 28.5g; Fat 23g, of which saturates 11.4g; Cholesterol 43mg; Calcium 715mg; Fibre 15.5g; Sodium 1120mg.

Currant bread
Krentenbrood

Makes 1 loaf

500g/1¼lb/generous 4 cups strong white
  bread flour, plus extra for dusting
2 sachets easy-blend (rapid-rise)
  dried yeast
250ml/8fl oz/1 cup lukewarm milk
50g/2oz/¼ cup white caster
  (superfine) sugar
pinch of ground cinnamon
pinch of ground nutmeg
pinch of powdered saffron
1 egg yolk, lightly beaten
50g/2oz/¼ cup butter, softened, plus
  extra for greasing
10ml/2 tsp salt

For the filling

150g/5oz/⅔ cup currants
150g/5oz/1 cup raisins
50g/2oz/⅓ cup finely diced
  glacé (candied) citron peel
50g/2oz/⅓ cup glacé (candied) orange peel

Cook's tip
Before rolling up the dough at the end of
step 3, shape 200g/7oz almond paste into
a roll, place on the dough rectangle, roll up
and continue as above.

Per loaf Energy 3375kcal/14303kJ; Protein 57.3g;
Carbohydrate 705.8g, of which sugars 324.8g; Fat
55.2g, of which saturates 28.6g; Cholesterol 308mg;
Calcium 1098mg; Fibre 26.2g; Sodium 4651mg.

For many centuries the bread eaten by Dutch country people was
dark rye bread. White bread was a luxury, hence the Dutch expression
wittebroodsweken, literally "white bread weeks" for a honeymoon. Even
more luxurious was white currant bread. Bakers all over the country still
take great pride in baking it, especially for the weekend and festivals such
as Christmas and Easter. Much longer currant breads are baked in the
region of Twente, situated in the eastern part of the country, where the
birth of a baby is celebrated with a 1.5 metre/1½ yard loaf.

1 Sift the flour into a bowl and make a
well in the centre. Add the yeast and a
little of the milk to the well and mix
together, incorporating some of the flour.
Add 5ml/1 tsp of the sugar, cover the bowl
with a clean dish towel and leave to stand
for 10 minutes.

2 Add the cinnamon, nutmeg and saffron
to the remaining milk, add to the bowl and
mix well. Add the egg yolk, the remaining
sugar and the butter and knead briefly,
then add the salt.

3 Turn out the dough on to a lightly floured
surface and knead vigorously for at least
15 minutes, until the dough is no longer
sticky and is full of little bubbles, adding
a little extra milk if necessary.

4 Shape the dough into a ball, return to a
clean bowl and cover with a dampened dish
towel. Leave at room temperature for
1 hour, until it has doubled in bulk.

5 To make the filling, poach the currants and
raisins in plenty of simmering water for
10 minutes. Drain well and pat dry in a cloth.

6 Turn out the dough and knead in the dried
fruit and both types of glacé fruit peel. Dust
both the dough and the work surface with
flour and roll into a rectangle 30cm/12in
wide. Brush the flour away on both sides.
Roll up the rectangle, starting at the top or
bottom, wherever the filling is most sparse.

7 Grease a 30 x 10 x 10-cm/12 x 10 x 10-in
loaf tin (pan) with butter. Place the dough roll
in the tin, with the final fold underneath.
Cover with a dampened dish towel and
leave at room temperature for about 1 hour,
until the dough has just risen above the rim.
Preheat the oven to 200°C/400°F/Gas 6.

8 Bake the loaf for 35 minutes, then brush
the top with cold water and return to the
oven for 1 minute. Turn out on to a wire rack
and leave to cool.

Further reading

de Moor, Janny "Dutch Cookery and Calvin", in: H. Walker (ed.), *Cooks & Other People* (Proceedings of the Oxford Symposium on Food and Cookery 1995), pp.94–105 (Prospect Books, Totnes, 1996)

de Moor, Janny "Dutch Farmhouse Gouda: A Dutch Family Business", in: H. Walker (ed.), *Milk: Beyond the Dairy* (Proceedings of the Oxford Symposium on Food and Cookery 1999), pp.106–116 (Prospect Books, Totnes, 2000)

de Moor, Janny, Nico de Rooij, Albert Tielemans, *Het Kookboek van de Eeuw*, (Kosmos Z&K, Utrecht, 1999)

Jansen-Sieben, Ria and van der Molen-Willebrands, Marleen, *Een Notabel Boecxken van Cokeryen*, first published c. 1514 (De Kan, Amsterdam, 1994)

Jobse-van Putten, Jozien, *Eenvoudig maar Voedzaam: Cultuurgeschiedenis van de Dagelijkse Maaltijd in Nederland* (Sun, Nijmegen, 1995)

Pagrach-Chandra, Gaitri, *Windmills in my Oven: A Book of Dutch Baking* (Prospect Books, 2002)

Riley, Gillian, *The Dutch Table: Gastronomy in the Golden Age of The Netherlands* (New England Editions Ltd. (London, 1994)

Schama, Simon, *The Embarrassment of Riches: An Interpretation of Dutch Culture in the Golden Age* (Fontana Press, London, 1987)

van Dam, Johannes and Witteveen, Joop, *Koks en Keukenmeiden* (Nijgh & van Ditmar, Amsterdam 2006)

van der Meulen, Hielke, *Traditionele Streekproducten: Gastronomisch Erfgoed van Nederland* (Elsevier Bedrijfsinformatie, Doetinchem, 1998)

van Otterlo, Anneke, *Eten en Eetlust in Nederland 1840–1990: Een historisch-sociologische Studie* (Uitgeverij Bert Bakker, Amsterdam, 1990)

van Winter, Johanna Maria, Van Soeter *Cokene: Recepten uit de Oudheid en de Middeleeuwen*, (Unieboek, Bussum, 1976)

Willebrands, Marleen, *De Verstandige Kok: De Rijke Keuken van de Gouden Eeuw* (Pereboom, Bussum, 2006)

Witteveen, Joop and Cuperus, Bart, *Bibliotheca Gastronomica: Eten en Drinken in Nederland en België 1474–1960*, 2 vols. (Linnaeus Press, Amsterdam, 1998)

Suppliers

The Netherlands:

Marqt
Utrechtsestraat 17, 1017 DA Amsterdam
Tel: +31 20 820 4285;
www.marqt.nl

Gimsel
Mariniersweg 9, 3011 NB Rotterdam
Tel: 010-4046597;
www.gimselrotterdam.nl

Realdutchfood.com
Lennondreef 8, 5012 AT Tilburg
Tel: +31 6 24617799;
www.realdutchfood.com

Hollandshopper
Paardelanden 10, 7925 PK Linde
www.hollandshopper.nl

mail order:
www.typicaldutchstuff.com
www.hollandsbest.eu

United States:

A Touch of Dutch
11 Front St NW, Coupeville, WA 98239
Tel: (360) 678-7729; Toll Free: (888) 772-4855;
www.atouchofdutch.com

Dutch Corner Restaurant
3154 Main St, Manchester, MD 21102
Tel: (410) 239-8100;
www.dutchcornerrestaurant.com

Vander Veen's Dutch Store
2755 28th Street SW, Wyoming, MI 49519
Tel: 1-800-813-9538;
www.thedutchstore.com

Nelis' Dutch Village
Corner of US-31 at James 12350 James Street, Holland, Michigan 49424
Tel: (616) 396-1475;
www.dutchvillage.com
www.godutch.com

North American Dutch-owned businesses
Holland American Bakery
246 NJ-23, Wantage, NJ 07461z
Tel: (973) 875–5258;
www.hollandamericanbakery.com

mail order:
www.thedutchshop.comTel: (416) 247-8659;
hollandstore.wixsite.com

Canada:

The Dutch Market
80 William Street South, Chatham, ON N7M 4S3
Toll free: 1(866) 355-1351; (519) 352-2831;
www.dutchmarket.ca

Holland Store
2542 Weston Road, Toronto, Ontario, M9N 2A6
Tel: (416) 247-8659;
www.hollandstore.ca

New Zealand:

New Zealand:
Go Dutch Shop (food, gifts)
10 Hillary Square, Orewa Tel: 09 427 8477 and
385 Great North Road, Henderson, Auckland
Tel: 09 836 6211;
www.godutchshop.co.nz

Karikaas Natural Dairy Products
156 Whiterock Road, Loburn, Rangiora,
RD2 7472, North Canterbury
Tel: + 64 3 3128 708;
www.karikaas.co.nz

Australia:

The Dutch Shop
Shop 5/121 James Street, Guildford WA 6055
Tel: 08 6278 1888;
also at: t Winkeltje
85 Market St, Smithfield NSW 2164
Tel: 02 9604 0233;
www.thedutchshop.com.au

It's All Dutch to Me
Unit 13, 291 Wickham Road
Moorabbin VIC 3189
Tel: 0433 446 350;
www.itsalldutchtome.com.au

The Dutch Pantry
72 O G Road Klemzig
Adelaide, SA
Tel: 8261 1095;
www.thedutchpantry.com.au

Index

Publisher's acknowledgements

The publishers would like to thank the
following for permission to reproduce their
images (t=top, b=bottom, l=left, r=right):
p6bl Alamy; p6br Allen Collins/alamy; p7tl
Picture Partners/Alamy; p7b Robert Harding
Picture Library/Alamy; p8 Paul Almasy/
Corbis; p9t Peter Horree/Alamy; p9b
Christie's Images/Corbis; p10b The
Bridgeman Art Library; p10t PCL/Alamy;
p11b The Print Collector/Alamy; p11t Neil
Setchfield/Alamy; p12bl Eddy Linssen/
Alamy; p12br John Van Hasselt/ Corbis;
p13t Owen Franken/Corbis; p13b Mary
Evans Picture Library/Alamy; p14 Hulton-
Deutsch Collection/Corbis; p15t Peter
Horree/Alamy; p15b David Sanger
Photography/Alamy. All other photographs
© Anness Publishing Ltd.